Fiqh 112

Five Pillars (Ḥanafī)

Version 2

Student Handbook……………………………………………………….	**p. 1**
Tayba Instructors…………………………………………………………	**p. 4**
Tayba Contact List………………………………………………………..	**p. 5**
"Ascent to Felicity" Companion Text……………………………………..	**p. 20**
Guide to Hajj……………………………………………………………...	**p. 105**
Fatwa on Friday Prayers in Prison………………………………………..	**p. 143**
Information on Tayba Foundation………………………………………...	**p. 144**
Curriculum Map…………………………………………………………..	**p. 155**
Course Assignments and checklist………………………………………..	**p. 156**
Student Question Form…………………………………………………...	**p. 166**

STUDENT HANDBOOK

FIQH 112 Five Pillars (Ḥanafī option)
Version 2

Instructor: Tayba Faculty

Welcome to this Tayba Foundation course. We realize the unique and difficult situation our students are in (such as lack of money, high security, changing of locations without notice, solitary confinement, etc) and we will accommodate any reasonable situation for a student who sends us a written explanation. If you feel unable to complete the course for any reason, contact us to see if we can help - *Tayba Faculty*

This handbook is designed to provide the information you need to help you complete the course. It is split into three sections, please read them all carefully:

1. Course information
2. Advice on studying for this course
3. Assignments and grades

Course Information

FIQH 112 is a correspondence course. To succeed in this course, you must be proficient in managing your time well and being self-motivated to go through the material and ask questions when you need to.

Course Description

This course is based on the famous text *Marāqī al-Saʿādāt* (Ascent to Felicity) of the Egyptian scholar Abu al-Ikhlas Hasan ibn Ammar al-Shurunbulali al-Wafa'i - otherwise simply known as al-Shurunbulali due to his central role in disseminating the Ḥanafī School. For the purposes of this course, we will be using the wonderful translation of Shaykh Faraz A. Khan. However, since we will be building on FIQH 111 and will only be covering the pillars of worship, we shall skip the first and last few chapters. Since Faraz A. Khan has already supplied an ample amount of footnotes in his translation, this coursebook will not be like the previous coursebooks. Instead of providing a full commentary ourselves, this coursebook will act only as a supplement, to be read in tandem with the White Thread Press edition. After you have completed this course, in sha Allah, you will have learned the basics of what you need to know with respect to worship according to the Ḥanafī Madhhab.

Course Objectives

The student will meet the following learning objectives:

1. Understand and fulfill completely the rituals of ṭahāra, ṣalāh, ṣawm, zakāt and Ḥajj according to the Ḥanafī Madhhab.
2. Acquire the skill of self-guided study using multiple resources in order to enhance one's understanding of the religion and study ability

Instructors

There are a number of instructors who contributed to developing this course, as well as being available to answer questions and grade your assignments at the end of the semester. Please see the supplementary information at the end of this course book to read their biographies.

Communication between Students and Instructor(s)

TAKE ADVANTAGE OF YOUR INSTRUCTORS!

We now have three permanent instructors on staff; Lumumba K. Shakur, Abdul-Muhaymin and Abu Hamza. **We made these additions in order to ensure that ALL of you have access to someone who can competently assist you in your studies.** You can contact Tayba instructors by email, phone (collect call) or by written letter. We expect everyone to contact their instructors throughout the semester as a regular part of their study process.

QUESTIONS & ANSWERS

Remember that all Tayba instructors can be reached via email or written letter at "instructors@taybafoundation.org" using whatever email system your facility has partnered with. You can register us as your contact on your CorrLinks, JPay, GTL, or JailFunds account using "instructors@taybafoundation.org". For those who don't have email access, we can still be reached via letter.

Any questions you may have should be submitted in writing. We have found that asking questions over the phone quickly burns through the limited time that we have with you, while written questions allow issues to be properly researched and referenced for everyone's benefit.

We encourage you to send in your questions during the term by phone, mail or email. If sending mail is difficult, or you do not have the option to send an email or make a call, then please send in all questions along with your coursework submission as a last resort. Please note that <u>questions about the course should ***not*** be submitted with your course assignments</u> unless you have no other choice. All questions should be submitted separately, throughout the course of the term.

By email: For questions regarding the course material or assignments, you can email instructors@taybafoundation.org via CorrLinks, JPay, GTL, or JailFunds, if those services are available to you. When sending mail, always include "FIQH 112" in the subject line of the message.

By letter: Please briefly include the subject of your letter on the envelope, for example "FIQH 112 question about assignment". This will help us to respond to your letters more quickly. You may use the Student Question Forms found at the back of this book.

Please be sure to write your **name and ID number** on all communication with Tayba Foundation, particularly on all of your assignments.

By phone: Phone access has always been part of the package of services provided with every course, so please call us collect. Please see the contact list of phone numbers below.

You may also consider giving the message to a family member or friend with whom you are in contact. That person could then email us or phone us and we can answer an inquiry if you give them permission to receive information on your behalf about your studies.

TAYBA FOUNDATION
Freedom Through Education

www.taybafoundation.org

You can register us as your contact on your CorrLinks, JPay, GTL, or JailFunds account using "instructors@taybafoundation.org". If you are calling by phone, please call us collect. All of our instructors are remote team members and do not work in the California office, so please pay attention to the office hours and time zones, as well as each instructor's course assignments listed below.

Lead Instructor: Ustadh Lumumba K. Shakur

Phone: (510) 491-7859
Email: instructors@taybafoundation.org
Office Hours: Monday to Friday, 9 am to 5 pm EST | Saturday & Sunday (by appointment)

Courses taught 2022-2023: IMAN 100 | FIQH 100 | FIQH 101 | FIQH 111 | ADAB 101 | FIQH 102 | FIQH 112 | ADAB 102

Instructor: Ustadh Abdul Muhaymin al-Salim

Phone: (510) 641-8881
Email: instructors@taybafoundation.org
Office Hours: Monday to Thursday, 8 am to 2 pm EST | Saturday & Sunday (by appointment)

Courses taught 2022-2023: IHSN 101 | SIRA 101 | USUL 101 | IMAN 101 | QRAN 101 | HDTH 101

Instructor: Ustadh Abu Hamza Daniel Archuleta

Phone: (510) 491-6165
Email: instructors@taybafoundation.org
Office Hours: Monday to Friday, 9 am to 3:30 pm EST | Saturday & Sunday (by appointment)

Courses taught 2022-2023: FIQH 121 & FIQH 122

Tayba Contact List - all departments
Information for Students

Tayba Department	Email	Phone
General		
Office / front desk	N/A	510-952-9683
Academy		
Instructors general student inquiries	instructors@taybafoundation.org	N/A
Lumumba - Lead Instructor	N/A	510-491-7859
Abdul Muhaymin - Instructor	N/A	510-641-8881
Abu Hamza - Instructor	N/A	510-491-6165
Life Skills		
Life Skills general student inquiries	lifeskills@taybafoundation.org	510-952-9875
Reentry		
Reentry general inquiries	reentry@taybafoundation.org	949-627-0718
Student and Reentry Coach	james.h@taybafoundation.org	510-641-8882

 31080 Union City Blvd, Ste 208, Union City, CA 94587   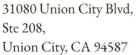 1 (510) 952-9683   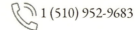 info@taybafoundation.com

Academic Dishonesty

The Tayba Foundation's Student Code of Conduct and Honor Code strictly prohibits any form of academic misconduct, such as plagiarism or cheating on exams. Academic misconduct is an unacceptable activity in scholarship and is in conflict with academic and professional ethics and morals. Academic misconduct may result in a failing grade and/ or expulsion from the program.

Course Schedule

A key to success in a correspondence class is to keep up and not get behind. The deadlines listed below are designed to help you succeed in this class by encouraging you to keep up with your work throughout the semester. You are free to submit your work before the final deadline, however please note that tests and papers will **NOT** be graded before the deadline. You will receive a postcard confirmation in the mail once we have received your work. Submit all tests and the term paper together.

Suggested timeline to keep up with the coursework:

Spring Term (March 1 - June 30)	**Fall Term** (September 1 - December 31)
March: Lessons 1-3	September: Lessons 1-3
April: Lessons 4-6	October: Lessons 4-6
May: Lessons 7-9	November: Lessons 7-9
June: Lessons 10-12	December: Lessons 10-12
June: Submit all assignments together	December: Submit all assignments together

The final deadline to submit the exam and assignments is June 30th for the Spring Term and December 31st for the Fall Term.

If, for any reason, you are unable to submit the coursework on time, please provide a brief note explaining the reason for late submission.

Advice for studying for this course

In terms of the motivation to study, it should suffice us that Allah ﷻ has honored knowledge and its people in His Book. Allah ﷻ has said:

(Are those who know equal to those who do not? Nay they are not equal) (Qur'ān 39:9)
(Ask the people of knowledge if you do not know) (Qur'ān 16:43)
(Only the scholars have deep fear of Allah) (Qur'ān 35:28)

Also, the many sayings of the Messenger of Allah ﷺ should be enough to motivate us to desire to seek knowledge such as, **"Seeking knowledge is incumbent on every Muslim." (Ibn Majah)** In imitation of these two Divine sources, we find much praise about the stations of knowledge. For example, Imām Mālik when he was asked, "When does studying become blameworthy?" He answered, "When does ignorance become praiseworthy?" Because of the vital importance of knowledge, we have made *The Instruction of the Student* by Imām Zarnuji one of the first courses in our curriculum under the name "ADAB 100: How to Study Islam". For those of you who haven't taken it yet, it is composed of an original translation and brief commentary of Imām Zarnuji's work by Shaykh Rami Nsour with a new updated collaborative commentary that is geared specifically towards distance learning.

NOTE: Those who took this course prior to the Spring 2017 update can still benefit from study advice in this new edition by reading this section of the handbook. The method of study we describe below was summarized from that new edition of the course. **So if you have already taken courses with Tayba Foundation in the past and have not yet read this revised "Advice on How to Study" please do not skip it.**

Traditionally, the Islamic method of learning began at age seven lunar years with memorization
of the Qur'ān. During that time students would also acquire the necessary tool of the Arabic Language. Then they would go on to study Islamic Creed ('aqīda), Islamic Jurisprudence (fiqh), Arabic Grammar (nahw), Foundational Methodology (uṣūl) and many other sciences. All the texts that were studied were committed to memory, as this was one of the main ways of preserving the knowledge. Even if a person did not have access to his books for whatever reason, whether they were stolen or destroyed, the river of knowledge continued to flow. Even though memorization is a vital part of any advanced study program, we will not focus on that aspect of learning in the early phases. What is most important at this phase in your religious education are two things: developing good study habits and learning Arabic. We will start with the second one first.

The Importance of Studying the Arabic Language

Traditionally, religious texts were studied one-on-one with a teacher who would give the commentary orally and guide the student during the course of their studies. But due to the unique circumstances you all are faced with, most of you do not have access to a teacher who can do this. So we decided to try a new method. Just like when water is not available for ablution (wuḍū'), one does dry ablution (tayammum) as an inferior, but necessary alternative. So in addition to the core Arabic texts, we have provided a translation along with either our own commentary or a transcript of a lecture on the text delivered by someone who is qualified to teach it, written in a style that is like you are sitting with us in a classroom.

Through this method, we hope that you will use the texts as a way of both learning the subject and increasing your understanding of the Arabic language. Without the Arabic language, you will never gain a deep understanding of Islām. Historically, Arabic was studied by students after creed ('aqīda), jurisprudence (fiqh) and purification of the heart (tazkiyat al-nafs). But those were for people who could already read Arabic. In places where Arabic was not the spoken language of the land, it was learned simultaneously with other disciplines. So even though Arabic is ranked behind other sciences, truly understanding all other disciplines in our Din rests entirely upon your developing a functional mastery of the language.

Many people exert all effort to another language in pursuit of a woman or to acquire a job. Where are those that will learn Arabic for the love of Allah ﷻ and His Messenger ﷺ? For those who don't already know Arabic and are in places that do not offer Arabic classes, a good book series to start with is the 3 volume set called *The Arabic Course for English Speaking Students* by Dr. V. Abdur Raheem. This series is otherwise known as "The Medina Series" because it is used by Medina University in Saudi Arabia and is one of the most common textbooks used to teach Arabic to non-Arabic speaking people. (NOTE: For those of you who are wondering, Tayba is working on offering an Arabic course in the future. Please stay tuned.)

If you study our texts in the suggested manner found below, we are sure that you will greatly increase in knowledge of the Arabic language while at the same time learn the knowledges that Allah has obliged us to know. And Allah knows best. We have seen a number of students who knew little to no Arabic go through a text like *Mukhtaṣar al-Akhḍarī* with a basic book on Arabic grammar and within a few months acquire a grasp of the language using our method of study.

But first you have to be able to read the Arabic alphabet. If you are not at this level, you should work on getting to this point while you go through our courses in English initially. Once you have mastered the alphabet, go back and review the text again. It will only further improve your comprehension of the material and help build a functional Arabic vocabulary. To help with this, we have attempted to translate many of our texts as literally as possible so that you can more easily see what is going on when you begin working with the Arabic text directly.

Once you are ready to work with the Arabic, you should begin by writing out a few lines of the main text in your own handwriting into a notebook. This will serve as your personal copy of the text, an Arabic workbook where you can practice your grammar and an eventual manual for you to use if you decide it is time for you to memorize the text once you have progressed sufficiently. It is much easier for you to memorize anything from handwriting than it is memorize it from a typed version. Typed Arabic looks exactly the same and may be more pleasing to the eye, but handwriting causes slight variations that will help your brain preserve the text better. This is why most Qur'ān schools still use chalkboards called a "lawh" to help Qur'ān students memorize. Similarly, there are a growing number of educators in the West who argue against removing chalkboards from classrooms because they are a type of interaction that computers and tablets cannot replace. Because you do not have a chalkboard, it may be helpful for you to have two notebooks: one that is simply a copy of the Arabic text and another that you use for the grammatical breakdown/personal notes. Having two notebooks will have the added benefit of giving you a central place where all of what you have studied is kept, while giving you the option to pull your individual notebooks when you need to review or teach others the material.

One man who was guided and greatly benefited from a version of this method was our American martyr (shahid) El-Hajj Malik El-Shabazz—otherwise known as Malcolm X. He says in his autobiography in chapter 9, "Saved":

I spent two days just riffling uncertainly through the dictionary's pages. I'd never realized so many words existed! I didn't know which words I needed to learn. Finally, just to start some kind of action, I began copying.

In my slow, painstaking, ragged handwriting, I copied into my tablet everything printed on that first page, down to the punctuation marks. I believe it took me a day. Then aloud, I read back, to myself, everything I'd written on the tablet. Over and over, aloud, to myself, I read my own handwriting.

I woke up the next morning, thinking about those words- immensely proud to realize that not only had I written so much at one time, but I'd written words that I never knew were in the world. Moreover, with little effort, I could also remember what many of those words meant.

Malcolm, may Allah have mercy on him, began this process after being frustrated over not being able to express himself in the English language, as his mother tongue was the slang of the streets. The end result of his efforts was a man who was so eloquent and educated that he could hang with professors who had attended the most elite universities the world had to offer. For those that are frustrated over the inability to access the Arabic language, this process will benefit them as well.

As you write down the text and begin to break it apart, you will slowly start to see what is going on with the sentence structure, vocabulary and how meaning is conveyed. Learning Arabic is about gradual, consistent practice. So take a little of the core text at first and slowly increase the amount you work through as your comprehension improves. Look at every word and figure out what it means by looking at the translation and using a good dictionary like "Hans Wehr" (known as *The Dictionary of Modern Written Arabic*) to understand why we made that translation choice. One of the brilliant decisions that Hans Wehr made when he composed his dictionary was to order it based on the trilateral roots of any given word. So unlike other dictionaries, you cannot just look up the word as it is written. You have to look up the root and then find the form of the word you are looking for under that entry in the dictionary. This forces you to break words apart, while simultaneously getting you accustomed to the ways in which the root words give meaning. Hans Wehr is the first step to any English-speaking Arabic program, whether it is in the madrassas of South Africa or religious seminaries in Texas. So please do not disregard the type of learning you will acquire simply by using it as a dictionary. (NOTE: If you do not know how Arabic works yet, you will not understand what we mean. *In sha Allah*, you will as you start to learn the basics of Arabic grammar.)

After you have broken down the Arabic as much as you can manage, you then start to work with the commentary. *In sha Allah*, this will be familiar to those of you who have taken the Spring 2018 (and beyond) edition of ADAB 100. For those who have not, what follows is essentially a cliff notes version.

How to Study Islam: The "Pearl" of ADAB 100

Though we actually describe two methods of study in ADAB 100, we will only focus on the second method here for the reasons we explained above. In ADAB 100, we have nicknamed this second method "The Eastern Method" and it has four steps: (1) review, (2) preparation, (3) examination and (4) follow-up.

After you have worked on breaking down the Arabic, you will then transition into crafting your notebook into a personal commentary. When you sit down to study (if you are not beginning a text for the first time), you should begin by reviewing the previous day's material, reading at least the core text (matn) and ideally your notes before you move on to the current section you are about to study. This will help anchor the previous material in your mind and refresh your memory about things that may be connected to the current lesson.

You then prepare for the current lesson by writing out the Arabic text in your notebook, reading the translation and writing down any questions that come to your mind. When you get to more complicated texts, you may even need to read the passage a few times before moving on to the next step. A lot of advanced works are written in a cryptic manner (*e.g.*, *Al-Mukhtaṣar* of Imām al-Quduri and Sidi Khalil in the Ḥanafī and Mālikī Schools respectively) or their subject-matter requires a little bit more time to dissect (*e.g.*, formal logic [mānṭiq] and theology [ʿaqīda]) and so you will have to read them over and over again before you understand what the author is saying. This is where the Arabic breakdown we advised in the beginning becomes so important.

After you have made your preparations, you then turn your attention to the commentary and examine the text, thoroughly reading and digesting what is explained there to the best of your ability. Also keep in mind that some of our courses technically offer two distinct commentaries of the same text. Please do not just pick one to read and skip the other. We have given you both of them for a reason. Again, when reading through the commentary, if you feel that you need to re-read certain passages, then do not feel ashamed to. Half of learning is repetition. **Most importantly: take notes**. Our scholars say "The hand teaches the heart" and you will remember much more of what you have written with your own hands than you will of what you have merely read. This is also where you should look at the questions you wrote down beforehand and see if they were answered in the commentary. If not, you should research them afterwards and may even find the need to pose your question directly to us if you are unable to find an answer. **But please, don't just ask us every question that you have written down. You should be able to figure out some things on your own and the process of research will ultimately teach you much more than you will learn by simply asking us to spoon feed you the answer.** Though it is natural to ask a lot of questions in the beginning, as you progress in your studies, you should eventually be able to find the answers to most issues with just a little guidance. So you may find sometimes that we don't directly answer your question, but pose another question to help you think it through yourself. This is because the entire point of an Islamic education is to produce men *and women* who are competent enough to both read and properly apply the scholarly legacy that has been passed down to us from the previous generations. This means thinking like a scholar and not simply being a collector of information.

The end result of all of this should be that personal commentary we spoke of earlier. This will be the thing you review and can use later to teach from. This latter point is important because teaching something to another actually forces you to master the material in a much more comprehensive way than personal study requires. That is because people think differently and the individuals that you are sharing the material with may have questions that you never thought to ask. So you should not feel shy about teaching the course material to others, whether it be one-on-one instruction with someone who is not yet a Tayba student, group study sessions/book clubs or Friday khutbas you have been tasked to deliver. Teaching is an important part of learning. **NOTE: This does not mean that you have formal permission to teach anything on Shaykh Rami Nsour's or Tayba Foundation's behalf. Formal authorization is a grueling process that is now no longer an official part of our curriculum.**

After you have studied your daily portion of the text, you should follow-up by reading the core text again, tie up any loose ends and note any any parallel articles or works that may have been recommended in the lesson to help you increase your knowledge of the subject. For example, a lot of people complain that students of fiqh who study a madhhab do not focus enough on the Qur'ān and Sunna. *This criticism is completely valid.* Though we should not interpret the Qur'ān and ḥadīth on our own, this does not mean we should not read them with reverence and passion. So for example, while you are going through our fiqh series, you should also be reading works like *Al-Muwaṭṭā'* of Imām Mālik, *Miskhat al-Masabih* of Khatib al-Tabrizi, or *Bulūgh al-Marām* of Ibn Hajar al-Asqalani (depending on the particular madhhab you have chosen) that were written to supplement fiqh studies. Regardless of the subject, you may find that reading ḥadīth collections will allow you to make connections between relevant verses or aḥadīth (plural of ḥadīth) and the material you are currently studying. More importantly, you will benefit from the Qur'anic or Prophetic advice contained in such passages that may not have necessarily been the central focus of the text.

The follow-up phase is also where you should do any detailed research that may help explain things that caught your interest, could potentially resolve some issue you or the community may be facing, give you a place to gather the textual proofs or reasoning (legal or rational) behind a particular issue or include further details that were hinted at in the commentary in your notes. This is also why scholars refuse to answer students questions sometimes, because it is obvious from the question that follow-up has not yet been done. So do not be surprised if the answer to your question is "Go back and look at such-and-such section". That being said, we understand that you have limited resources, but far too many questions we are asked are about things that are actually answered in the course book (or will be answered in the next level of the subject when it can be better appreciated).

Once you have improved your Arabic to such a level that you can start to read things independently, your follow-up may include reading parallel commentaries of the same text. So for a student on the Mālikī track who can read Arabic, even though Shaykh Rami has explained everything you need to know in *Mukhtaṣar al-Akhḍarī*, he will usually instruct you to start over and go through a work called *Ḥal al-Masā' l fī Sharḥ Mukhtaṣar al-Akhḍarī bi-l-Dalā'il*. This work is a lot more academic than Shaykh Rami's explanation that has been aimed at beginners and discusses the textual proofs of the legal rulings mentioned in the text. <u>NOTE</u>: This is important because sometimes people are against classical teaching methods and the very idea of following a legal school, but what the classical scholars are doing is a gradual education (tarbiya) where students are exposed to things when they have been properly prepared to handle them. So when it comes to the tiresome debate over so-called "blind-following" Tayba's response to this question is "Why should scholars be blamed for people who do not read the works where the proofs have been explained?"

This follow-up phase is what separates average students from burgeoning scholars. The Syrians say "A faqīh who doesn't read at least 8 hours of fiqh a day is not a faqīh." So in Syria, a student of fiqh, once he or she has mastered the language of the discipline, will pick up a fatwa collection and just start reading it cover-to-cover. Once complete, they will find another fatwa collection and start the process over again. Most of what they read may not be relevant to their situation, but if they come across an important statement, they will write it in their notebook and that becomes part of their personal repertoire. Through this constant review and follow-up, they may not memorize works word-for-word, but their brains are being trained to remember where to find the answers that they need and are slowly absorbing little bits of information along the way. And this constant reading helps condition their brain to think like the scholars of the past. This is why the scholars of ḥadīth can read a ḥadīth in Arabic and tell that it is a fabrication without even analyzing the chain of transmission. Through their constant reading of authenticated narrations, they pick up on the Prophet's ﷺ way of speaking and they develop a link with the Prophet ﷺ that they sometimes refer to as recognizing his "fragrance" and can tell immediately when his fragrant scent is absent from a statement.

(And those who strive in Our (cause), We will surely guide them to our Paths...) Qur'ān 29:69

This is the path to mastery. It takes time and effort, but if you persevere you will be victorious, *in sha Allah*. Knowledge is precious and Allah ﷻ will only let you have it if you struggle. Even for the Messenger of Allah ﷺ, revelation was received only after experiencing great pain. At the first revelation, the Angel Gabriel, squeezed him three times and then our Messenger ﷺ began reciting. Each squeeze was unbearable, but he was being shown that knowledge can only be received by those who endure hardship. In the story of our Masters Moses (peace be upon him) and Khidr (peace be upon him as well), when the former was going to seek knowledge from the latter, Moses (peace be upon him) said, **(We have become tired because of our journey)** (Qur'ān 18:62) *I.e.*, his quest for knowledge was sometimes exhausting.

One must struggle to gain knowledge by staying up late into the night or getting up before dawn. Imām Shafi'ī said, "Whoever seeks lofty things will stay up late at night. Whoever seeks lofty things without struggle will have wasted his life seeking the impossible. The one who seeks pearls dives into the [depths of the] ocean." Similarly, El-Hajj Malik El-Shabazz said when recounting the long hours he spent reading every night, "That went on until three or four every morning. Three or four hours of sleep a night was enough for me. Often in the years in the streets, I had slept less than that." With this in mind, you must also recognize that your body has a right over you, so give it rest from time to time. Traditionally, schools set aside two days a week for rest. During this time, the students would pursue personal interests, spend time with friends or do other light study.

We hope that for those that receive this book are now set on a lifelong journey of seeking knowledge. This process will include moving from this text to other texts on the subject—going from beginning primers, to intermediate works and then on to the advanced texts. The same goes for all the other subjects (*e.g.*, 'aqīda, uṣūl, sīra, fiqh, logic, *etc.*) And as we alluded to, we also have a contact system for those that are going through the text, so that they can clarify anything that is obscure. This system is "The Tayba Distance Learning Program for Islamic Sciences".

With this as a beginning, we hope to increase the number of Muslims who have a deep understanding of the Dīn who can then move to spreading the correct message of Islām. If we want the best for ourselves and our families, we must strive to get this understanding, or fiqh. Our Master Muhammad ﷺ said, "Whoever Allah wants good for him, He will give him deep understanding (fiqh) of the Dīn."

We ask that Allah ﷻ accept all of our actions and gives us success in following the way of our Master Muhammad ﷺ. We ask all those that receive this book to pray for those who aided in putting the study package together and for their families and teachers.

Summarized Advice on How to Study This Course Material

1. Take a short section of the text, write out the Arabic, work on deconstructing the language and then study the commentary we have provided. Don't forget to review the previous lesson.
2. Read and take notes on ALL the material that is found in the text, whether it is a published book, audio transcription or supplementary article.
3. Keep track of any questions you may have, research the answer and send any you are unable to resolve to Tayba in writing. Please make sure you mention the course name and edition in the letter (*i.e.*, "FIQH 112, v2").
4. Follow-up your lessons by doing additional readings related to the subject matter. Please note that we are not always able to provide additional resources to students, but are more than happy to make recommendations.
5. Lastly, use any additional methods of study that you have found beneficial to master the material. Every student will have different methods that they have developed or learned which works for them.

Essay Writing Made Easy - a Student Guide

All essays should have an *introduction*, a *body,* and a *conclusion.* A balance of these 3 sections is important. A good rule of thumb is:

Introduction: 10 %   **Body:** 80 %   **Conclusion:** 10 %

Helpful Tip: Before you dive into your essay, create an outline to help organize your thoughts.

Step1:

The first thing you need to do is answer your topic or research question.

For example: **How has the knowledge you have learned from "The Abridgement of Al-Akhdari," affected your personal, family, and community life?**

- Ask yourself what topics, from the text, will you reflect on? Wuḍū', Tawba, Ghusl, Prayer etc.
- Think about how the knowledge you have learned has affected your personal, family, and community life.
- Ask yourself some specific questions: (for example)

- How has the act of tawba changed my life with my parents?
- After learning the importance of ghusl, how has it changed my understanding of cleanliness?
- How has the act of promoting good and forbidding evil affected my relationship with the brothers in my community?

Step 2:

In this step you want to narrow your ideas further. An average essay will make a general statement of what was learned and briefly mention what effects it had on your life. A **strong** reflective essay will:

- State what was learned
- State how it has affected an area of your life
- Provide personal examples
- Give an insight to the outcome

(Example)

1. Promoting Good and Forbidding Evil
    - Give a brief statement on what this means
    - Discuss how you tried to implement what you learned
    - Give examples of the success or obstacles you encountered
    - Provide an insight as to why you encountered problems
    - Talk about how it made you feel

Step 3:

Create a thesis

This is probably the most important part of the essay. Every essay must have a thesis statement. The thesis statement is one or two sentences, in your **introduction**, that contains the focus of your essay and tells the reader what the essay is going to be about. You want to make sure your thesis piques the interest of the reader.

(Example of Average thesis)

1. *"For the purpose of this essay I will talk about wudu, tawbah, and ghusul and how they have affected me in my personal, family, and community life."*

This thesis is correct. But it is also unimaginative.

(Example of an interesting thesis)

1. *"Knowledge is the key to freedom," is a statement I have heard throughout my life. I have never truly understood its meaning until I began studying sacred*

knowledge. What I have learned has had a profound effect on all areas of my life. **(Then you can list the topics you will discuss)**

This thesis pulls the reader into wanting to read further to find out what the author has to say. Don't worry if a thesis extends a little beyond the two sentence norm. Sometimes you need to build up to what you want to talk about.

Important Note: Now that you've organized what your thoughts and ideas are you can start your essay.

Introduction

The introduction is the first paragraph and the point of entry for your essay. It is where you will introduce your thesis.

Body of the essay

The body of the essay is where you will discuss your three points. Each paragraph will focus on one topic. To make your paragraphs effective follow these guidelines:

Paragraph 1, 2, & 3

- Topic sentence
- Supporting sentences
- Concluding sentences

    1. The **topic sentence** introduces the point you will talk about.
    2. The **supporting sentences** provide details to support the topic. Use examples, your opinion or personal accounts to give more value to your topic.
    3. The **concluding sentences** sum up what you've said in the paragraph and pave the way for your next topic sentence.

Conclusion

Your conclusion is your last chance to highlight your point of view to your readers. The impression you create in your conclusion will leave a long lasting effect with your reader long after they've finished the essay. The end of an essay should bring a sense of completeness and closure to your discussion.

Final Note

A strong essay is not just well organized thoughts and ideas. It is also important to pay attention to spelling, grammar, punctuation, and vocabulary.

Basic Grammar Rules

- For every sentence, your subject and your verb need to be in agreement. The most common mistakes are with the verb "to be."

subject	present	past
I	am	was
He	is	was
She	is	was
It	is	was
You	are	were
They	are	were
We	are	were

- Only use capital letters for proper nouns and at the beginning of a sentence. Proper nouns are specific names of people, places or things.

Common Noun	Proper Noun
teacher	Murabit al Hajj
city	Los Angeles
document	Declaration of Independence

- When a sentence is complete use appropriate punctuation.
- Sentences should be complete thoughts and not fragments. For example: (*fragment*) **went to the ballpark**. *(complete)* **He went to the ballpark.**
- Do not use double negatives. Double negatives are two negative words used in the same sentence. For example,
    - That won't do you no good.
    - I ain't got no time for supper.
    - Nobody with any sense isn't going

Vocabulary

A rich vocabulary is important for effective writing. Refrain from using slang words.

diss	disrespect

bling	jewelry
ain't	is not

Final Thought

Writing takes practice. The more you write the better you get. If you have any questions or concerns, the Tayba staff is here to help.

Course assignments and grades

Assignments that you must complete

There are **five assignments** that you must complete, and one bonus assignment that you may complete if you wish. Details for each are found at the end of the book.

1. Essay
2. Compare and contrast project
3. Fasting pamphlet
4. Zakāt pamphlet
5. Create a diary, letter or diagram map on performing Ḥajj
6. ***Extra Credit*** Ten scenario questions

Assignment deadline

The final deadline to submit the exam and the writing assignment is **June 30th** for the Spring Term and **December 31st** for the Fall Term.

Please note that any assignment received AFTER the due date will NOT be read. It will be refused and will only be graded the next semester. This is to assist our graders in grading assignments in a timely fashion, as a better service to our students. We ask that you please respect the deadlines.

If, for any reason, you are unable to submit the coursework on time, please provide a brief note ***with as much notice as possible*** (before the deadline) explaining the reason for late submission and we will evaluate the eligibility of a late submission at that time.

You are free to submit your work before the final deadline, however please note that assignments will NOT be graded before the deadline. You will receive a postcard confirmation in the mail once we have received your work.

A reminder that any questions you have must be submitted throughout the course term and not sent in with your assignments.

Submit all assignments together. **DO NOT SUBMIT THEM SEPARATELY**.

USE BLUE OR BLACK INK ONLY.

Preface to the *Ascent to Felicity* Companion

It is our intention that you read this companion with your reading of the individual chapters of *Ascent to Felicity* as printed by White Thread Press. It would be better if you read it after or while reading instead of before since we are trying to help you contextualize the work as it has been written. We have followed Sh. Faraz Khan's chapter names and subsections and so reading this companion after will be much more natural. We hope that it will aid your comprehension, as well as perhaps clear up a few things that may not be entirely clear or written according to the paradigm as the previous work, *The Beginner's Gift*, which was the subject of the entry-level course. In contrast to *Tuhfa al-Mubtadi*, *Maraqi as-Sada`at* is a relatively early work and so its organization is not as strict as latter works. Since this work is typically studied a little later in a traditional curriculum, we will hopefully provide some of what you may be missing which someone who has studied more intensively would have naturally picked up along the way. We also have kept in mind the specific circumstances that are unique to our students which Shaykh Faraz Khan would naturally have not considered when he was writing his footnotes. We hope that this companion helps to make the work particularly relevant to our students and address most of the daily concerns that you may have which the typical student who is going through this work may not. Since we are filling in information, there may not be a direct correlation between one sentence and the next. One sentence may be addressing something in the text, while the next may be addressing an unrelated footnote. Therefore, we shall use bullet points in order to indicate that a different subject is being discussed. This is why we would like you to read this companion alongside or after the text, since much of it will not make sense if you read it prior.

Many institutions opt to skip this work in preference for other titles and do not read Imam Shurunbulali until they get to *Nur al-Idah*, whereupon this particular work becomes like a summary review text. But since it better fits with our curriculum and has been translated and commented upon by someone who both has mastered the text and is a native English speaker, we have decided to use it instead of other alternatives that are usually preferred. Also, in order to get you used to reading classical texts, we will often refer to Imam Shurunbulali as "our author" and Shaykh Faraz Khan as "our commentator" in order to make a distinction. This, you will commonly find in classical texts, especially those that contain marginal notes which supplement the commentary that has been written by another scholar. This "companion" is actually like a marginal commentary (hashiya), only as a result of us being unable to add these notes to the published editions of this work without permission, we have been forced to write it as a separate document. So we hope that it will help train you on how to read and navigate the expositions of two different commentators who are simultaneously addressing the same text. In sha Allah, you will come across this frequently in your advanced studies once you transition to reading texts in their original Arabic.

Given that this is our first iteration of this course, we will be continually improving, revising and developing it as time goes on. If there is anything which you come across that is unclear in the main text, footnotes or our companion commentary, please bring it to our attention so we can attempt to resolve it for you and include it in future versions of this companion piece.

Islamic Creed

As we said, since the focus of this work is on the personally obligatory knowledge (fard ayn) as it relates to worship, we will skip this chapter for the time being. However, you should know that Imam Shurunbulali modeled this chapter off of the famous work *Aqida al-Tahawiyya* that is the subject of IMAN 101. It therefore provides an excellent review text of that work. This is especially true given the nature of Sh. Faraz Khan's footnotes, which were largely drawn from classical commentaries of the *Tahawiyya* itself or commentaries of works like the *Jawhara al-Tawhid* which will likely be the core text around which IMAN 201 is based. If there is anything unclear about this chapter, please see what we have said about the topic in IMAN 101. You will not be tested on this section of the text.

Purification (Tahara)

"Purification is valid with the following types of water…"

- Unlike the other three schools who came after them, the Hanafis categorize water differently. Instead of judging water based on its color, taste or smell, they ask the basic question "Can we still simply call it 'water'?" This is because the hadith "Nothing can make water impure unless it alters the water's smell, taste or color" (Ibn Majah, Bayhaqi, Tabarani) is weak.[1] As the commentator says in the footnote, this means that if you can call something "water" without further qualifications, it is considered pure and purifying in the Hanafi school. So "rose water" or "lemon water" or "iced tea" are not fit to be used for purity since they have been "conditioned". In the event that something pure is added to water that may be odorless or colorless or has no smell, whether or not the water remains purifying would then depend on whether or not enough of this other substance has been added to alter the water from its essential "water-ness". In this case, if the volume or amount of the other substance is more than the water itself, then the water is considered to have been "overcome" by the other substance and so it is treated like a "watered-down" version of this new substance and is no longer considered to be water. As Imam Mawsili says in his *Al-Mukhtar li-l-Fatawa*, "Purification is not permitted with water that has been overcome by something [else such] that [it] lifts the essential nature of water – such as drinks, vinegar, and rose water. This overcoming is considered by volume."

Please continue on the next page. The gap below is necessary in order to keep the diagram which follows from getting split between pages. If you see any more gaps like this in the FIQH 112 Companion, assume that the same thing has occurred.

---

[1] Even though it is weak, it is an example of a weak hadith that the scholars have agreed to act upon it. Imam Shafi`i, for example, acknowledges this weakness and says "However, its meaning is agreed upon by everyone and I know of no one who disagrees on this matter. Unlike the other three Schools, the Hanafis only consider it unfit if <u>two</u> characteristics have been changed out of consideration for the narration's weakness. This is why our author refers to it being free from something that can "condition" it.

FIQH 112: PURIFICATION (TAHARA)

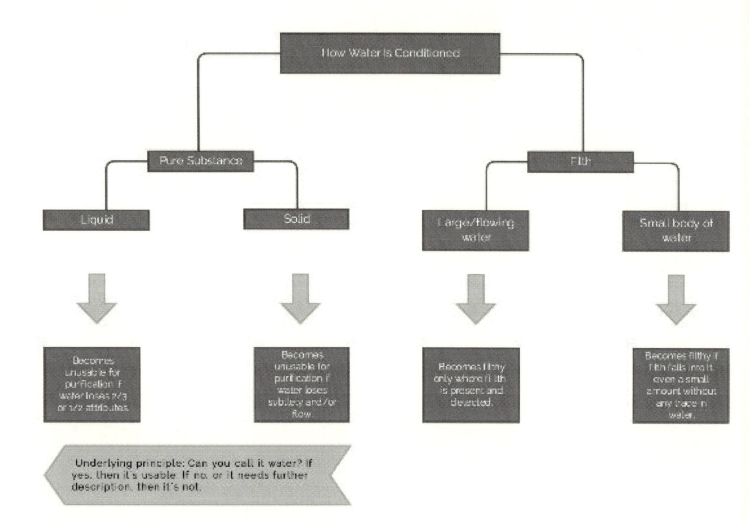

- <u>NOTE</u>: Doing diagrams of this nature is highly recommended by our scholars as a way of helping you to visualize and summarize the subject. We therefore recommend that you create charts like the above, along with tables and graphs for every chapter in this book in order to help you understand it is as much as possible. The only reason we have not done this for you more frequently is that it would make certain parts of the assignments too easy.
- When removing impurities, the Hanafis only give consideration to the impurity being removed. So the removal of impurity in the Hanafi School is not limited to "unconditional water" (ma mutlaq) as it is with the other Schools, but any pure liquid. Thus, Imam Mawsuli states a little later in the same work "It is permitted to remove filth with water, and also any pure liquid - such as vinegar and rose water." And so the complexities and debates over certain modern phenomenon with respect to water are not an issue for the Hanafis - *al-hamdu li-Llah*. "Tap water" is unquestionably water, even though it contains traces of chlorine. It is still considered water by custom. Even though the chlorine smell may be noticeable, as well as a slight taste, if someone asked you for a "glass of water" and you gave them water out of the tap, would anyone think that you gave them anything but "water"? That is the standard by which you can

measure what "water" is in the Hanafi School. With respect to washing machines, you need not worry. Since it would be valid for you to wash your clothing in Kool-Aid, soapy water is not an issue in the slightest.

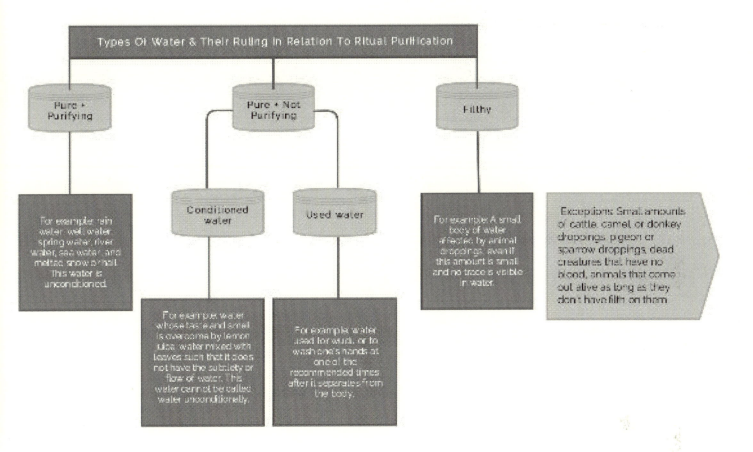

ABLUTION (WUDU')

"The obligatory integrals of wudu are…"
- The "top of the forehead" is the point at which a normal hairline begins. If someone is bald or balding, the length of their face remains at where their hairline would have been. This is only a technical point however, since if you washed more than this, it would not be a problem in the Hanafi School.
- "Washing" means that enough water must be used that it drips off of the limb. Anything less than this is considered wiping and does not fulfill the obligation. So whether you "bring water" to your limbs with a cupped hand or you stick them under the faucet, it does not matter, as long as water drips off of the limbs that need to be washed.
- In terms of the commentator's statement "Hence, one may not wipe over hair that hangs below the ears, even if tied up above the head; rather, the hair that is wiped must grow out from above the ears." What he

means by this is if someone has very long sideburns that they tied up into a ponytail, those hairs are not considered "the head", but "the face" and so it would have to be washed and not simply wiped over.

"Among the emphasized sunnas of wudu are…"
- The fact that the intention (niyya) is an emphasized sunna in the Hanafi School means that the intention is not required for wudu to have been affected. Therefore, the Hanafis state that if someone does any sort of washing with the intention of "worship", then it suffices for wudu. The most common example is washing your hands prior to eating. Since the Prophet (Allah bless him and give him peace) recommended this, when you do this, then your hands are considered to be "washed" when it comes to wudu. So as long as you don't do anything to break your wudu, when you "formally" make wudu, you could already consider your hands to have been washed since the Hanafis also give no consideration to continuity in terms of the legal validity of wudu. Therefore, "washing the hands up to and including the wrists in the beginning of wudu" has already been taken care of, even if done 20 minutes prior. This isn't necessarily important in terms of practicality, but is important in understanding the difference between something being an obligation or a sunna in an act of worship.
- Likewise, since continuity is a sunna mu'akkada and not fard or wajib, you still should wash your hands again when making wudu if a long time has passed. However, continuity in wudu becomes very important when you get to the chapter on wiping over khuffs. Skipping a sunna mu'akkada is only sinful when done intentionally and habitually. If it is done circumstantially, then it is not sinful and continuity is not a consideration. Therefore, if you were prevented from completing your wudu due to some emergency or the cell block being locked down, once it is over, you should continue where you left off. How this relates to wiping over khuffs, we will discuss when it becomes relevant.
- Wiping the back of the neck is established through several ahadith. Although they are weak, many of the Hanafi scholars did not consider them weak enough to not act upon. Therefore, the commentator clarifies that the stronger opinion is that doing so is mandub and not a sunna.

"Among the etiquette of wudu are…"
- "Adab al-Wudu" in later texts of the Hanafi School are referred to as either "light" Sunnas, mandub or mustahhab actions.
- "Facing the Qibla" and the rulings related to it apply in the "open air" when there is no wall or structure around you by the consensus of all scholars. However, doing so inside buildings seems to be the apparent opinion of Abu Hanifa as well. If your sink is positioned in such a way where facing the Qibla while making wudu is difficult, then try to turn at least your chest and face towards it as much as you reasonably can. The same applies to when you are using the bathroom. If you can avoid facing or putting one's back directly to the Qibla while answering the call of nature, then you should out of deference to the Hanafi School. But if it is difficult to do without maintaining your privacy or cleanliness, then turn away as much as you reasonably can.

"Among the things disliked in wudu…"
- "Wasting water" applies to the water that actually hits your limbs and it is why drinking the leftover water after your wudu is recommended. If you can make wudu out of a container, it would dramatically reduce the amount of water that you use. If that isn't possible, just make sure that the tap is only slightly turned on so that it runs lightly over your limbs and is not splashing everywhere.

FIQH 112: PURIFICATION (TAHARA)

- "Having someone else assist" in case it is not clear from the commentator means having someone wipe your limbs for you. It does not mean someone cannot pour the water or bring it to you. The only time someone should assist you in your wudu is if you are bedridden or have some sort of injury that makes it difficult for you to properly perform wudu when performing it with water would not cause any further damage (*i.e.*, you threw your back out and you have a hard time bending over to wash your feet).

- "The legal reason for performing wudu…" is a reference to the actual intention that you should make prior to performing wudu. A lot has been said about this and much of it is overly complicated. To simplify this issue: make wudu with the intention to pray. The intention itself is a simple matter that new students frequently make unnecessarily complex. The best that I have heard in this regard is one of my teachers who commonly asks rhetorically "Are you making wudu or are you eating a hamburger?" Just as our intention when we put our shoes on to go outside or lay in our bed to go to sleep is obvious, the niyya is that simple. It does not become complicated because it is deen-related. When you approach the sink, know that you are washing your limbs so that you can pray and do not worry about anything else that you have read or may have said. Even stating one's intention aloud is only recommended in the Hanafi school for people who are affected by waswasa. It is not the normal ruling. When you approach the sink, are you washing your hands so that you can eat dinner or are you washing your limbs so that you can pray dhuhr? It is a simple question with a simple answer.
- "Ability to perform the prayer"… this means that if someone is in a "Gulag" prison where they are chained to the wall and prevented from practicing religion or live under a place like Spain after the Reconquista where praying would get you killed, the ability is not there. In any other situation, even if you are not necessarily able to stand and prostate (due to the cellblock being on lockdown for an extended period of time), if you can make prayer with head movements, then wudu is required.

"The conditions of validity of wudu are…"
- "The removal of anything that blocks water…" anything that blocks water, whether it be nail polish for women or caked on mud for men, must be removed. The only exception, as the commentator mentions, is for someone who works with materials that make doing so impractical. In the opinion of our scholars, this would include so-called "breathable" or so-called "halal" nail polish that some people have claimed is permissible to wash over for women. In the Hanafi School, water must "flow over" the limb and it is hard to argue that water flows over fingernails that have been painted on merely because a bit of moisture may eventually leak through. Anything that is not essential or unavoidable must be removed. If it is not unavoidable, (*i.e.*, grease for mechanics, glue for carpenters, *etc.*) then you must remove as much as you reasonably can.
- "The ending of any state…" this simply means that anything which breaks wudu has stopped prior to your beginning it.
- "Obligatory… Touching a verse of the Qur'an" the Hanafi School has the strictest opinion with respect to the Qur'an. Anything that is intended to serve the Qur'an, they extend the prohibition of touching the Qur'an to that thing. So while other Schools consider it permissible to touch a translation or tafsir without wudu as long as you do not touch the actual Qur'anic text, the stronger opinion in the Hanafi school is that touching a translation or tafsir are both impermissible without wudu as mentioned in footnote 78 by the commentator.

- "Recommended… to avoid disagreement of scholars of other schools of thought" this is known as "mura'atil al-khilaf" in which positions that are more precautionary are followed from other Schools in order to ensure maximum validity, especially in acts of worship. Here, making wudu would be recommended after touching a woman out of deference to Imam Shafi`i or after a man touching his private parts out of deference to Imam Malik.

"Wudu is nullified by any one of the following.."
- "Anything that exits from the two openings" there is no consideration given to the nature of why it exited in the Hanafi School, even if that thing is considered pure or the result of a medical condition, like tapeworms.
- "Filth that flows" means anything that leave the point of exit that is filthy nullifies wudu in the Hanafi School. The easiest way to test is if you have a small cut that isn't "running", wipe the blood away and if it comes back and begins to form a drop, your wudu is broken. The same with puss. This also means that if you have a cut, the previous condition of "the ending of any state that contradicts it while washing" would apply. Unless you have a wound that is continuously bleeding or you have a blood condition that causes you to have a problem clotting, you have to wait until you stop bleeding before you can make wudu and pray. If your bleeding won't stop, then you follow the ruling of someone affected by a chronic condition.
- "Sleeping in a position such that the buttocks are not firmly planted" since it is not physically possible to pass gas in a position with your buttocks firmly on the ground or in a chair without intentionally contracting your muscles, which will not happen in your sleep.

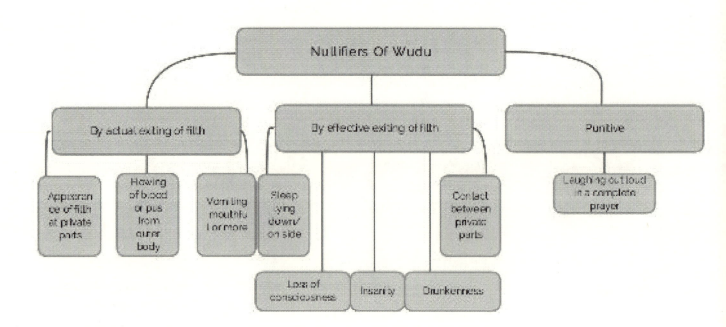

- We understand from all of this that merely touching impurity does not break one's wudu. This is a misconception that many Muslims unfortunately have.

FIQH 112: PURIFICATION (TAHARA)

THE PURIFICATORY BATH (GHUSL)

"The following three actions are obligatory integrals of ghusl…"

- "1, 2 & 3…" means that ghusl in the Hanafi school is a very simple matter. After you rinse your mouth and nose a single time each, you pour water over your entire body, making sure you wet everything that is possible without difficulty and your ghusl is legally valid and complete. Everything else mentioned are the things which should also be done and not intentionally neglected. But if you rinse your mouth, nose and wet your entire body, you have made ghusl.

"Ghusl is of three types…"

- "The emission of sperm/sexual fluid that leaves its normal place inside the body with pleasure [even if it exits without pleasure]…." This latter phrase in the brackets "even if it exits without pleasure" means that if one ejaculated, but performed coitus interruptus (or pinched one's urethra to keep anything from exiting) and temporarily delayed the emission of sperm, once it eventually exits, ghusl becomes obligatory because the occurrence of that sexual fluid was the result of pleasure and its emission was merely delayed. This also means that if one suffers from a medical condition in which sexual fluid is emitted without any sexual activity, it does not does not place one into a state of junub in this situation.
- "Mandatory, namely, for someone who becomes Muslim while in a state of major ritual impurity"… *I.e.* if you converted after puberty and did anything to would place you in a state of junub, ghusl would be fard upon you immediately after taking your Shahadah.
- Everything else that is recommended if and when you are already in a state of major ritual impurity. If you awake from a wet dream, for instance, and it is jumu`ah time, then you would be required to make ghusl before you can pray. So your obligatory ghusl would also cover the recommendation if doing it after Fajr. And the recommendation of ghusl for Jumu`ah begins during the "day" of Jumu`ah, not the night before in the Hanafi School.

Obligatory Ghusl

1. Emission of Sexual Fluid
2. Sexual Penetration
3. Completion of Hayd & Nifas

Necessary Ghusl

1. Conversion of Islam by an Adult

Recommended Ghusl

1. Morning of Jumu`a
2. Prior to attending Eid
3. Entering Ihram
4. Day of Arafa
5. Entering Makka
6. Enter Madina
7. Ziyara to the Messenger (Allah bless him and give him peace)

FIQH 112: PURIFICATION (TAHARA)

- "Intercourse with an animal…" the fact that it doesn't require ghusl without the emission of sexual fluid does not mean it is not a major sin. This is just a technical point that clarifies that the hadith related to this was a reference to human beings. Nothing more should be read into this.

DRY ABLUTION (TAYAMMUM)

"Tayammum is permissible when…"
- "Being roughly one Hashimi legal mile…" meaning that you cannot simply make tayammum because it is not currently in your possession. If you have to purchase it, then you purchase it.
- "Extreme cold" meaning that you are exposed to the elements and fear that making wudu or ghusl would cause hypothermia or one of your limbs, fingers or toes to freeze.
- "Sickness" that is serious and which bathing would cause further illness or for healing to be delayed. The same would apply to water that is contaminated and is too dangerous to use for bathing or cleaning.
- "Lack of apparatus" *i.e.*, when water may be technically available, but unreachable as is the case of a well without a bucket (or when the tap is shut off).

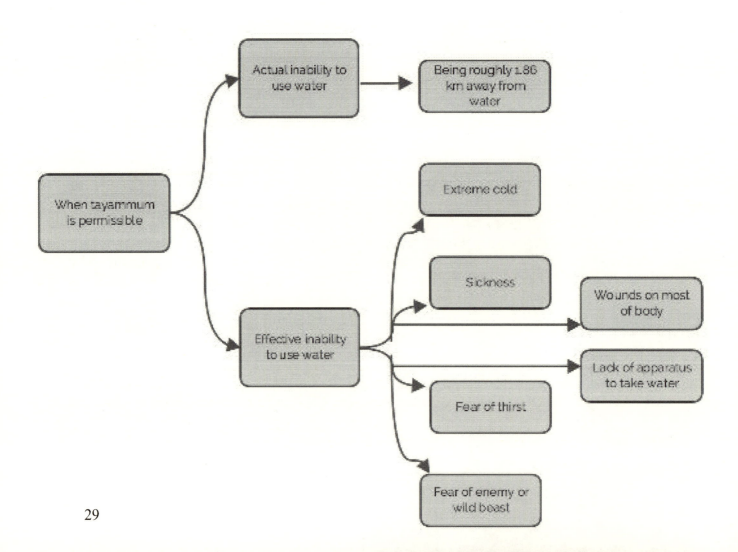

- **"Tayammum may be performed with any pure substance of the earth…"** that is in its natural state. Baked brick would be excluded along with grass or bark unless it has composted and degraded back into soil.
- "[E]ven the dust on clothes" *i.e.*, in desert climates or excessively dusty environments. In places like Pakistan or the Gulf, dirt blows constantly and it is possible that enough dirt has blown around to cause your clothing to be physically "dirty". In the United States, outside of remote deserts in States like Arizona where excessive dirt may whip around, this would not be relevant for most people.
- "Hence when a Muslim intends…" as the commentator says, the niyya is obligatory in tayammum, and tayammum is not valid without it. Also, tayammum actually removes the state of ritual impurity in the Hanafi School and so it is treated just like wudu and is valid until the excuse that permitted it no longer exists.
- "If one has wounds on his body, yet his uninjured limbs are more…" meaning that we do not mix wudu/ghusl and tayammum. If there is not enough water to perform a complete wudu or ghusl, we do not do a partial wudu or ghusl and then complete it with tayammum. Similarly, if you have wounds that would be negatively affected by washing, you "wipe" with a wet hand as you would your head, as is mentioned by the commentator. "Wiping" in footnote 105 does not mean wiping with a dusty hand, but a wet hand while performing either wudu or ghusl.

WIPING FOOTGEAR (KHUFFS)

- "Khuffs" are not "socks", but refer to leather footgear that the Prophet and Companions used to wear. In the Hanafi School, the ruling of wiping over "khuffs" is extended to whatever shares the same qualities. The upshot of this issue is that modern dress and cotton athletic socks do not meet the conditions of wiping. The only type of non-leather socks which do meet the requirements of wiping without any disagreement are synthetic leather socks or waterproof hiking/diving socks that are designed to keep people's feet from getting wet rot while in the wilderness. If they are not waterproof, there is debate over them among contemporary Hanafi schoars and one should therefore err on the side of caution out of concern for the validity of one's prayer. The same applies to shoes. It is not valid to wipe over shoes unless they meet the conditions of wiping. Their having strings means they are not a solid structure and their requiring them potentially violates the condition of their staying up on their own. So wiping over most shoes and most modern socks are both doubtful at best and should therefore not be done.
- "The minimum required area" means only that this much must be wiped in order for one's wudu to be valid. However, one should not restrict themselves to this just as one should not restrict themselves to wiping ¼ of their head during wudu without sufficient reason.

"The following things invalidate the wiping of khuffs..."
- When one has a valid pair of khuffs that has been wiped over, the khuffs form a "protective barrier" over the purity of one's feet. So when wiping over them is no longer permitted due to one of the above reasons, one simply needs to wash the feet and put them back on again. Why? Because continuity is not a condition of wudu's validity. Therefore, when one has made wudu and wiping over khuffs has been nullified, the rest of one's wudu remains intact and you are like someone who was unable to complete

their wudu. Thus, one's wudu is merely incomplete, not invalid, until one washes their feet, as long as nothing has been done to nullify the wudu that has been performed over the rest of the limbs. The same applies to the case of someone who has wiped over shoes *that are permissible to wipe over*. Once they are removed, the foot has to be washed. I have unfortunately seen many people make wudu, wipe over their shoes and then remove them and pray. This is a complete misunderstanding of the fiqh of khuffs and any prayer performed like this is invalid and must be made up. Wiping over khuffs is a legal dispensation, not a legal trick to get out of washing your feet. In the prison environment, there is no circumstance that we have seen which would permit wiping unless one has received a pair of leather khuffs or waterproof socks in the mail.

It is Valid to Wipe Footgear When It:	It is Invalid to Wipe Footgear When It:
• Covers foot to the ankle • Made from leather or waterproof material • Thick enough to not show the skin underneath • Worn after the feet have been washed • Each pair is free from large holes • Time period has not expired	• Does not cover or stay above the ankles on its own • Does not rip apart when walking at least 3.5 miles • Is made from thin non-leather material that does not repel water • One (or most of one) "sock" has been removed • Time period has expired

"It is not valid to wipe a turban, cap, face veil or gloves."
- Because wiping over khuffs is a rukhsa (dispensation) that is an exception to the general rule. No analogies (qiyas) are made based on rukhas. As for the hadith which state the Prophet (Allah bless him and give him peace) wiped over his turban, they are all weak and their details differ, some mentioning that he wiped his head under his turban. The hadith describing him wiping over other things are even weaker and so if one has a turban, kufi or hijab on one's head, you have to at least wipe ¼ of your head. As for wiping over a niqab or gloves, it is completely invalid.

WIPING CASTS

- The only other thing that is permitted to wipe over are casts or bandages, based on need and hardship, when the wound cannot be directly washed or wiped over without causing further harm.
- "Like khuffs, [wiping] the cast does not require an intention" because wiping over casts takes the place of washing in the same way that tayammum takes the place of wudu. Wiping over khuffs and wiping over casts or bandages are not analogous and so the rules that apply to each are not the same. The detailed differences have been mentioned by the commentator.

MENSTRUATION (HAYD), POSTNATAL BLEEDING (NIFAS) AND DYSFUNCTIONAL UTERINE BLEEDING (ISTIHADA)

- Unfortunately, many men skip this chapter of fiqh since they think that it does not apply to them. However, men do need to know the details of this for two reasons: (a) they need to know when it is permissible and prohibited for them to have intercourse with their wives and (b) they need to be able to explain the fiqh of their menstrual cycles to their daughters. Men has always been taught this chapter in classical works, even if women may understand some things more intuitively. This chapter should not be skipped and if this subject in general was more normalized, some of the unfortunately harmful stigmas that have been adopted by Muslims in certain cultures related to human sexuality and anatomy would never have occurred. There is no reason for any Muslim girl to think she is bleeding to death when she has her first period and Muslims who refuse to engage in such subjects with their children should not complain when public school systems step in and do their job for them. Fathers should be able to explain any and everything they need to to their daughters. If they cannot, then they will get it from someone who can and that person may not necessarily agree with your moral or religious views.
- "...after the age of adolescence"... *i.e.*, any bleeding that occurs to girls during their adolescence is considered an illness and medical advice should be sought. Similarly, any bleeding that occurs after menopause has fully onset is considered to be the result of illness as well and is not treated like menstruation.
- "Its minimum is three days…" as the commentator says, it is not a condition that the bleeding be continuous. If bleeding occurs intermittently, it is included in the "days" of menstruation. Once it has stopped completely, ghusl is due and so women should not wait any additional time to make sure that it will not return. Anything beyond ten days (or 240 hours) in the Hanafi School is considered to be istihada. And even though the Hanafis are alone in this opinion, in Western medicine, a woman's period that lasts longer than 10 days is considered irregular and so the Hanafi opinion on this issue is actually closer to medical science.
- "If the bleeding is less than three days…" this means, as the commentator says, that women must keep track of their cycles: when bleeding starts, when it stops and the periods of purity in between. Without

FIQH 112: PURIFICATION (TAHARA)

keeping track of her cycle, a woman can easily miss obligations, such as prayer and fasting, or perform them when it's not permissible for her to do so. The rules of menstruation are more technical than simply not praying whenever there is blood and praying whenever there isn't. For example, menstrual "blood" is not always red or brown, but can be pink, yellow, and every colored discharge is considered blood in most instances. Similarly, sometimes bleeding that lasts less than three days can be the continuation of one's previous cycle and sometimes it is considered istihada. And finally, bleeding that goes beyond 240 hours is not menstruation, but istihada. In order to know when bleeding is really menstruation and when it is not, one has to keep precise record of changes in one's vaginal discharge. This includes the exact time it began, stopped and anything noteworthy about the color of the discharge. Most texts that cover the basics do not go into a great amount of detail, as is the case here. For more details, please consult more specific works like the wonderful interpretive translation of Imam Birgivi's by Hedaya Hartford and Ashram Muneeb.

- "The fasts must be made up…" *i.e.*, if she is someone who experiences intermittent bleeding (which often is the result of psychological stress or illness), when the bleeding stops, she immediately makes ghusl and prays. If it happened during Ramadan, she also makes up her fasts. If it then returns and is not considered istihada, the period of purity she experienced is retroactively considered to be menstruation. That being so, if she fasted, then her fasts would have to be made up since it has become retroactively invalidated by the reappearance of her cycle, even though she did not know it was her cycle when it originally occurred.

"The following things are also unlawful during menstruation…"

- We do not believe that a woman's menstruation is a "curse" or "punishment". She is ritually impure and so certain things are not permissible, but she is not "filthy" or in a "sinful like state". For this reason, she is actually rewarded for not praying and is in act of perpetual worship if she has the correct intention. Purity-wise, she is no different than a man who has had lawful intercourse with his wife and has become ritually impure thereby. The only difference is that she is unable to become pure until her menstruation has ended. Therefore, these things and these things alone are impermissible out of the sacrosanctity of what has been mentioned. She can still cook, clean and have sexual interactions with her husband as long as there is no direct skin-to-skin contact between her navel and knee.

FIQH 112: PURIFICATION (TAHARA)

Hayd & Nifas Prohibit

Entering Places
- Any Legally Defined Masjid

Sexual Activity
- Sexual Penetration
- Skin-to-Skin Contact Between the Navel and Knee

Acts of Worship
- Reciting the Qur'an
- Touching a Mushhaf
- Fasting
- Prayer

"If her period ends within ten days, she may not have intercourse except after…"

- Since she has to become purified by performing ghusl or tayammum. In terms of the prayer, this is out of consideration to her husband since after she has missed a prayer, she has delayed her ritual purification beyond what she should have and therefore her negligence or ignorance of the ruling is not reason for them to not engage in intercourse. In the case of the latter, she is like a woman who has not made ghusl after having sexual intercourse. Though making ghusl immediately after is recommended, it is not sinful for her husband to have intercourse with her again before she has become purified. If her period returns, even though she technically is considered to be on her period retroactively, they would not be sinful for having intercourse in the same way that she was not sinful for praying and fasting during her intermittent period of purity.

"If her period goes past ten days, it is permissible to have intercourse with her as soon as it passes the tenth day…"

- For the same reason mentioned above, which is even stronger here since any blood that returns is automatically considered to be istihada and there is no fear that she will return to an impure ritual state.

FIQH 112: PURIFICATION (TAHARA)

"The minimum duration of tuhr is fifteen days…"

- *I.e.,* if her bleeding has stopped and blood returns before 15 days elapsing, the resumed bleeding is considered to be from the "previous" hayd and added to her days of menstruation. 15 full days, or 360 hours, must elapse between two cycles of bleeding for them to be considered menstruation. If blood returns before 15 days have elapsed, the resumed bleeding is considered to be from the previous hayd, and added to her days of menstruation. If this new total number of days exceeds 10 and the woman is not a "beginner" (*i.e.*, this is not her first period), then she relies on the last "normal" cycle she had to determine how long her period should be. Anything in excess of the number of days she bled in her last "normal" cycle is now considered istihada, and she must repeat any prayers or fasts that were missed during this time (though she is not sinful). The number of days her previous period lasted is referred to as "her habit" (as it will be in the next line).

- "...except when establishing a standard menstrual habit…" *i.e.*, when a young woman has her first period, she does not yet know what her typical period will be. As the commentator explains, if she has continous bleeding, her hayd is considered to be 10 days and the maximum purity the remaining days of the month. If bleeding returns before the current month is over, it is considered to be istihada until the next month begins. The first day of the new month is then considered to be the first day of her hayd and she proceeds counting from there. During this second hayd, this rule no longer applies since 10 days has been established as her habit. At this point, once 15 days of purity have passed after this new menstruation period, any new bleeding is considered to be her hayd.

- *Maraqi al-Sa`adat* is a summary text. In more detailed works, the scholars divide women according to their menstrual periods as either: beginners, established or pregnant. The previous bullet applies to beginners. For women who have an established period, if their cycle exceeds 10 days, then like intermittent bleeding, anything past her last normal "habit" is considered retroactively to be istihada. For example, if a woman bleeds for 6 days during her previous cycle and she either saw a white discharge or dryness after checking with cotton, but she bleeds for 12 days this month, everything from days 7 is considered to have been istihada and she is responsible to make up both her prayers and fasts since she actually was not on her hayd. However, since she did not know this until after the fact, she is not considered sinful for missing them.

"Postnatal bleeding (or lochia) is defined as…"

- Unlike hayd, nifas has no minimum since this bleeding is the result of her uterus cleaning itself after giving birth. Most women do not experience periods during pregnancy, but even if she did, her nifas under three days would not logically be added to her previous period since the bleeding here is of a completely different nature than her hayd. All bleeding of a pregnant woman is considered to be istihada. Once 40 days of bleeding have occurred, everything after this is considered to be istihada and is treated like the occurrence of istihada during her normal period.

"The following cases are considered to be dysfunctional uterine bleeding…" *I.e.*, istihada.

- "Any bleeding of a pregnant woman…" the previous bullet point was to explain the rational reason why nifas has no minimum number of days. But the fiqh declares that if a woman has a period while she is pregnant, it is considered to be istihada in the Hanafi School, even if medical doctors recognize it as a legitimate period. Fiqh and medical science have different standards and do not always line up. Fiqh establishes norms, beyond which things are considered to be a hardship. So even though many women may routinely experience bleeding for more than 10 days, it is considered to be istihada regardless of what may be happening medically.[2]

"Dysfunctional uterine bleeding is like a continuous nosebleed…"
- Once istihada is established, it is treated like regular blood. But because a woman cannot control it as she can a cut on her arm, it is ignored and it follows the rulings of those who have chronic conditions which ordinarily nullify one's wudu (known as salas).

---

[2] For the benefit of our students, in sha Allah, I will try to briefly explain the medical difference between hayd and istihada. This is not something that most people actually know and it took me pouring through medical textbooks with my mother and discussing the issue back and forth before we together came to this conclusion. Her medical knowledge helped me to understand what was happening, but my knowledge of fiqh actually helped her contextualize what was written in her medical textbooks. Without both of our input, neither of us would have understood what was actually going on. In sha Allah, this is a small example of why our scholars say that scientists or doctors should be consulted by religious scholars on issues that require their expertise, but the ultimate judgement is not left to scientists or doctors who can only look at the issue from one perspective, but it is with the mufti who is able to contextualize the information according to what the Qur'an and Sunna point to of legal obligation. Even though my mother was a doctor, I helped her understand the medical aspect just as much as she helped me since this issue is not something that is even taught to doctors unless they are OBGYNs who exclusively deal with female reproductive systems and have to know the details in order to competently practice.

The difference between hayd/nifas and istihada is important to know because there are many Muslim women who feel guilty praying and fasting while they are still bleeding, even when they know what the scholars have said about their situation. I, for example, knew one woman who bled for 20 days every single month and despite many people trying to get her to act according to what the fiqh of her situation demands, she refused to pray while she was bleeding. That means that for 40 years, she missed 10 days of prayer every single month and potentially up to 10 days of fasting every single year if we go by the Hanafi School. If we go by the others, she has still missed 5 days and neither determination is something that should be taken lightly.

Menstrual bleeding (hayd) is the result of a woman's uterus shedding itself of the extra lining it had began to form after it realized that the egg was not fertilized. During this phase of the lining being built up, the walls of the uterus thin to facilitate the eventual growth and stretching of its walls that will occur during fetal development. When her body realizes that the egg has not been fertilized and it needs to try to get pregnant again next month, hormones are sent which cause the shedding to occur. Istihada happens when too much of this hormone exists in the body and the shedding starts to include part of the uterine wall itself. When this over-shedding occurs, the tips of the normal blood vessels in her uterine wall become exposed and these exposed blood vessels burst and begin to bleed. Therefore, istihada is not the same type of "material" that is being shed during her menstruation, but is the very same blood that would flow from a cut on her arm. For that reason, it is not and should not be treated like menstrual blood. Even if it appears to look the same, in reality it is not. And in my humble opinion, this is one of the miracles of the Prophet (Allah bless him and give him peace) since there is no way that he could have realized this in his time. This is not something that can be observed without dissection and most certainly could not have been known by an Arab man living in the 6th century. Regardless, in terms of the medical science, this transition from womb "material" to broken blood vessels may actually happen to some women at 12, 15 or 20 days. But the shari`ah has placed the limit at 10 (at least in the Hanafi School) for the sake of providing an objective standard by which all women can function day-to-day without undue hardship. So even if a woman were to test her istihada and discover that it is actual womb "material" and not normal blood, that does not matter. We act based upon the Shari`ah and even medical science acknowledges that this happening after 10 days is an irregular medical occurrence. So even when medical science outwardly "disagrees" with the Sacred Law, the wisdom of the Shari`a's rulings in treating it as though it is an illness is still justified by it. And this is why many scholars have found their proof and confidence in the truth of Islam through their study of fiqh, since every ruling in the Sacred Law makes sense and there is no way the Prophet (Allah bless him and give him peace) or his Companions (may Allah be well pleased with him) could have so consistently guessed about things like this and routinely come to such profound and astute conclusions about economics, politics and human psychology.

FIQH 112: PURIFICATION (TAHARA)

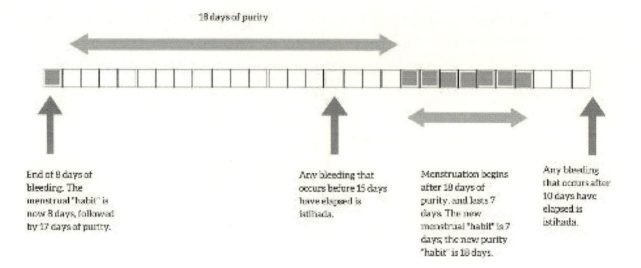

"There are three conditions for people with chronic excuses…"

- "The condition of establishing the excuse…" *i.e.*, if the nullifier of the wudu happens for the entire duration of the prayer time such that one cannot get through the prayer without breaking one's wudu (as is the case with gas and people who have weakened rectal muscles), what is mentioned in the text applies.
- "The condition of continuity…" *i.e.*, means that the excuse continues and so you make wudu and pray, without worry about trying to wait out the excuse.
- "The condition of its termination…" *i.e.*, means that once a prayer time occurs without the excuse occurring at least once, you must return to the normal situation and if it occurs again, it breaks one's wudu. You do not ignore the nullifier again unless it re-established itself for the duration of a prayer time again and the cycle starts over.
- <u>NOTE</u>: Many people unfortunately induce a chronic condition in themselves as a result of anxiety over impurities. Men are particularly susceptible to this, as the result of the curvatures of our anatomy. Anxiety subconsciously causes us to inadvertently close our urethra and trap a small amount of urine which eventually exits on its own due to gravity. The solution to this is to relax and stop stressing so much, particularly about urine. If you relax, your body will do its job and all of the urine will be expelled as it is supposed to. This is why it is common for medical doctors to prescribe anti-anxiety medications to men who complain about urinary incontinence (when it is not related to an enlarged bladder or muscular deterioration). You can also <u>lightly</u> apply pressure to your urethra in the space between your rectum and scrotum after you have passed as much urine as you can without straining yourself. Applying <u>a slight amount of pressure</u> at this point causes the natural vacuum in our urethra to expel any liquid that remains beyond that point. Since women's urethra is naturally point downward, they simply need to relax and make sure that they have emptied their bladders before they clean themselves after urination. Some scholars have also found that applying a slight amount of pressure in order to gently squeeze their bladder sometimes help push out the remaining urine in the same way that pressing against the urethra does for men.
- There are more details related to menstruation, postnatal bleeding and istihada, but these are the basics. Other works which treat the issue in more detail should be consulted in order to get a better understanding

FIQH 112: PURIFICATION (TAHARA)

of the nuances, particularly by our female students who necessarily need to know the details more than the men since you are the ones who have to actually implement them.
- NOTE: In terms of properly understanding this chapter of fiqh, we highly recommend the book *Birgivi's Manual Interpreted: Complete Fiqh of Menstruation & Related Issues* by Hedaya Hartfor and Ashrab Muneeb. It is unique in the way that it is structured and includes numbers charts and diagrams that would be too lengthy for us to try and replicate here. It also includes a particularly useful section that describe the modern ailments that relate to women's reproductive systems (e.g., yeast infections, painful discharges, etc.), why they occur and how to recognize them adopted from standard medical guides written for women to self-diagnose the less serious conditions that may afflict them from time to time.

TYPES OF FILTH AND PURIFICATION FROM THEM

"Filth is of two types: heavy and light…"
- "Wine" what is mentioned by the commentator is one of the two strong opinions in the Hanafi School. There is another opinion held by Abu Hanifa that non-grape alcoholic beverages are not impure. <u>This does not mean that they can be consumed</u>.
- Due to the proliferation of synthetic alcohol in modern cosmetics and beverages, many contemporary Hanafis have given the fatwa of purity for all alcohol that is not khamr (*i.e.*, grape wine). As a result, things like medicine, mouthwash and cologne/perfume are considered to be pure <u>when used for legitimate reasons</u>. However, the Hanafis are alone in this opinion.

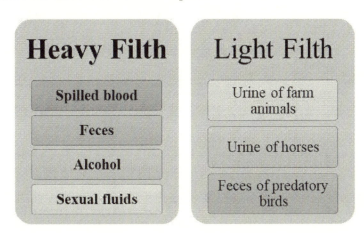

- The reason why there is a difference between the two is because there was a difference of opinion between the early Hanafi scholars over which substances were actually impurities. As a result, later Hanafi scholars took all of their opinions into consideration and included this substances that are difficult to avoid of being "light" filth and therefore excused in larger quantities.[3]

---

[3] This is also the case with non-grape alcohol, the purity of which was disagreed upon between Abu Hanifa and his Companions. Normally, Abu Hanifa's opinion is automatically given preference, but in this case, people began to abuse it in order to drink thinks like nabidh (spiced date juice) which is a drink similar to apple cider that can be either alcoholic or nonalcoholic depending on how long you allow it to sit. In order to prevent people from using

FIQH 112: PURIFICATION (TAHARA)

"A place with discernible filth on it is purified by the removal of the body of filth…"

- The "body of filth" is "ayn al-najasa" and once it is removed, it has been purified even if things like stains remain behind.
- "The amount of light filth that is excused is less than a fourth of one's entire garment…" this is a ruling that applies primarily to farmers who have to work with animals and cannot avoid getting their feces and urine on their body. Everything else other than these two things must be removed or the prayer is not valid if it is more than the size of a dirham.
- "A wet foot that steps on impure ground…" *i.e.*, ground upon which filth actually exists. We do not assume that an area is filthy without proof, even if it is a place where filth is likely to have come into contact with the floor (such as a hotel ballroom or kitchen floor). Despite it being likely that wine was spilled on the carpet during some time in its lifetime, we do not assume that any particular spot on the ground is filthy unless we have seen or can smell the filth presently there. This is because of the legal maxim "Everything is pure until it has been proven to be filthy" and the likelihood that the impurity was washed away with the routine cleaning that occurs in such places. The one exception would be the bathroom floor of a non-Muslim public facility, but in such cases, you can usually smell the urine. However, "smell" does not mean we put our nose to the ground, this is excessive. If an impurity is present, its odor will reach you where you stand.
- "Complete chemical transformation…" this applies most commonly to vinegar and solid soaps in the Hanafi School. Though lard (referred to as "tallow" in manufacturing) is used in the process, the addition of lye results in enough of a chemical change to render it pure in the Hanafi School. There are some people who apply this to gelatin, but this is a minority opinion that the overwhelming majority of scholars do not agree with. We, therefore, do not recommend any of our students follow this fatwa given the more than sufficient doubt over its accuracy.
- "The ground may be purified by drying…" applies only to the natural surface of the earth. It does not apply to tile, carpets, wood floors, etc. Even if someone urinated on the ground, once the urine has dried, that portion is considered pure for prayer.
- "A garment on one's body with dried sperm…" *i.e.*, because once it dries, what is there is the "ayn al-najasa" and once it is scraped off, like redness from a blood stain, it is ignored impure.
- "An exception is the skin of pigs…" *i.e.*, pig leather is intrinsically impure and cannot ever be purified. Therefore, if someone has pigskin shoes, they must be removed or the prayer is not valid. Purchasing them is unlawful, as is selling them. And because they are impure, it would not be permitted to wipe over them, even if they meet the other conditions.

Abu Hanifa's opinion as an excuse for drinking fermented nabidh, scholars began passing fatwa according to the other opinion. However, in our times, due to the proliferation of synthetic alcohol as a result of its properties as a binding agent of scents and flavors, many scholars have returned to Abu Hanifa's original opinion. And his opinion makes the most sense scientifically, since whenever sugar is present, you can be guaranteed that there is a trace amount of alcohol that is naturally created. This happens in virtually all fruits, drinks or breads. For that reason, as long as it is not abused, this opinion is acceptable to follow.

FIQH 112: PURIFICATION (TAHARA)

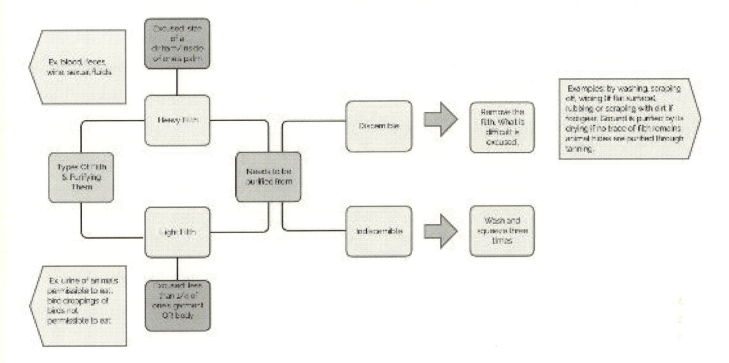

- Our overall attitude about impurities is that they have to be removed in order for the prayer to be valid. Otherwise, there is no real reason for us to be concerned about it. That is not to say that Muslims should not be clean, but we should not be obsessive in our cleanliness and someone who has impurity on their body is not in a state of sin. So there is no reason to "fear" impurity or develop anxiety over it. If a dog licks your hand, for example, we simply wash it off. If we work in the kitchen and have no choice but to cook improperly slaughtered meat or clean up after others who do, we simply put on our apron and get to work. The anxiety that many Muslims have over impurities is unnecessary and can lead to self-imposed waswasa.

WELLS

NOTE: Since this is not relevant in prison, we shall skip commenting on this section. Even if one's particular prison has a well system, they should also have a filtration system installed to ensure that the water is healthy and safe for drinking. This filtration system is sufficient to cleanse the water of any impurities in the same way as tap water is purified from the sewage and waste it is separate from at water treatment facilities.

TYPES OF SALIVA

- "This is the saliva of a human being whose mouth was clean…" *I.e.*, we understand from this that the saliva of non-Muslims, as long as it is not mixed with something impure which was in their mouth (like improperly slaughtered meat or alcohol), is pure. The verse in the Qur'an that describes the Mushriks as "unclean" is not taken literally.[4] However, there should be no reason why you should have to use leftover water that someone had drunk from for wudu, unless it is water that was given to you by your mother or siblings.

CLEANING AFTER RELIEVING ONESELF (ISTINJA')

- Istibra' is lightly "milking" the penis after urination to ensure that all of one's urine has exited prior to performing wudu. As we said above, in addition to what the commentator mentions, you can also lightly apply pressure (no more than the amount it would take to press a key on a keyboard or telephone) to one's urethra in the spot between the rectum and scrotum. Sidi Ahmad Zarruq mentions this and I have found it to be more effective than all of the other methods. And as we said above, women cannot do this in the same exact way. But instead, she simply empties her bladder, lightly presses on her bladder and waits a sufficient amount of time for all the urine to exit before she cleans herself.
- "If the filth does not move beyond the exit hole…" this is a reference to feces and by necessity, the amount of feces which remains on the rectum is excused, but sunna to clean. This is actually why the books refer to a "dirham" being the amount of filth that is excused, since the dirham is roughly the size of an adult's rectum. But referring to a dirham instead of the rectum is better adab in public.
- "If the filth moves beyond the exit hole…" again, a reference to feces and anything that spreads past the rectum must be wiped and preferably washed away.
- All this was a reference to feces, but can apply to urine as well. If men or women simply used toilet paper to remove the urine from the opening of their urethra, it would be sufficient. However, using water in addition to this is superior, as it helps to remove more impurity than dry substances on their own.
- As for your cell and the presence of the toilet in it, technically the entire cell would be considered a "bathroom" in the Hanafi School. However, due to the difficulty this would involve, you should simply avoid the area immediately around the toilet and try to pray, read Qur'an or make Dhikr as far away from it as you can (without being excessive). If you can cover the toilet (after cleaning its surface) with a clean towel when it is not being actively used, even better.

---

[4] Even by Imam Malik, who considers this verse reason to not allow non-Muslims to enter into the Masjid proper (*i.e.*, the legal definition of a Masjid which is discussed in the section `itikaf in the next chapter). However, even he does not consider the saliva of non-Muslims to be impure. So we can understand that even those Mujtahid scholars from the Salaf who took this verse literally, they still understood it to be primarily a "spiritual" or designation pointing to an unseen reality. Unfortunately, the common people in certain places where Muslims are the overwhelming majority of the population treat Christians and Hindus like their touching food or drinking from the same wells spoils the water. This is a bid`a. Many of "us" have the exact same attitude. We should not treat non-Muslims as though they are "filthy". As long as nothing that they eat or consume which we consider to be najis is spreads to us (by drinking water from the same cup immediately after your mother who may have been sipping on a glass of wine, for example), they are not "impure". And this attitude that we tend to we have often becomes a major barrier to Da'wah. Why would anyone be motivated to embrace a religion that considers them to be filthy for merely existing?

The Ritual Prayer (Salat)

PRAYER TIMES

"The times of the prayer are five…"
- We generally encourage everyone to learn how to determine the times of the prayer without reference to a calendar or an app. Though some of the prayers may be difficult to determine in prison, knowing the signs is something that is obligatory, while relying on calendars or apps *to the exclusion of the celestial signs* is impermissible by agreement. Pre-calculated calendars are good guides and apps are only beneficial if you first know which calculations to use as a basis. .The actual times of the prayer are established through the means mentioned in the text. Our scholars state that even if we use calendars as guides, they should be routinely tested against the actual methods of determining the prayer times to ensure they are accurate throughout the year. In previous times, Muslims developed sundials and other means to easily identify the times of the prayer (this is something that we encourage as well). In our times, mathematical calculations have been made the basis of many things, even though they are frequently less accurate than the Prophetic observational methods. That being so, they are an innovation in the same way moving toilets into the home or adopting the astrolabe in order to help predict the likelihood of lunar sightings were novel changes. They can be benefitted from, but only when we understand the limitations and complications that they produce. With respect to calendars, they give a false mathematical certainty to things that are based upon observation and therefore vary according to atmospheric conditions. As a result, they should not be taken as absolute and no one should pray or fast according to the exact second that they indicate.[1] However, because it is not always possible for you to physically observe the necessary phenomenon while you are incarcerated, relying on calendars sometimes becomes necessary. However, they still should be used as guides and not definitive determinations. You therefore should not fast or pray according to the very second that they indicate the prayer time has come in, but wait a few minutes in order to establish certainty. This is actually the practice of mu`addhins in the Muslim World anyway. In Syria and Morocco specifically, the callers to prayer typically wait a few minutes after they have visually confirmed that the prayer has entered in order to be absolutely certain that it is indeed time to pray.
- "The time of fajr (subh) is…" *i.e.*, in places unaffected by light pollution. Due to the existence of security lights around for the prison, determining the exact point at which Fajr enters is difficult, if not outright impossible. For fasting, this becomes problematic, but for the prayer, you can eventually tell when it is in if you have visibility of the sky. As the commentator indicates, in the Hanafi School, Fajr enters when the light "spreads" across the horizon and this is actually a little bit later than what most "standard" prayer calendars identify. The point at which the light first appears and remains on the horizon has been identified around 18 degrees, but the point at which it begins to spread has been identified as around 15

---

[1] As proof of the inherent problem of doing so, I have a computer, a phone and a tablet, two of which have the same app. For Fajr, for some odd reason, they all go off at slightly different times. Additionally, the primary astronomer at ISNA actually discourages using mainstream prayer calendar websites or apps and provides more accurate calendars upon request if he is given the exact coordinates of your city. Unlike the calendars and apps that are common among people, he takes into consideration atmosphere anomalies, temperature and other conditions which generic formulas cannot take into consideration

degrees. Visibly sighting this earlier time is not possible due to the security lights in the prison (and surrounding businesses in the area blocking out the natural light of the stars). But we are not sure if this latter time can be sighted either. The difference between the two in most places is anywhere from 30 to 45 minutes. This has implications for both fasting and prayer. Since you are unable to determine the time for themselves due to the circumstances of their incarceration, using an accurate calendar to judge the approximate times is permissible. But please keep in mind that this time is merely an approximation. So give yourself a little buffer. You should stop five minutes earlier than the calendar for fasting (imsak is 10 minutes anyway) and another five minutes after has entered for the Fajr prayer.

- "The time of zuhr is from…" *i.e.*, if one is at Makka or near the equator, you are unlikely to have much of a shadow when the sun as at its highest point. But if one is away from the equator, there will be a small shadow during most of the year. When determining the end of zuhr, the length of this shadow at the entrance of zuhr is added to the height of the object being used in order to determine asr's time. As for asr, there are famously two different times in the Hanafi School. Though the text seems to indicate that the earlier time is preferred, most Hanafis prefer the later time as argued by Abu Hanifa. This later time is attributed to a number of Companions, most noteworthy of whom are Abu Bakr and Abu Hurayra. So it is not Abu Hanifa's "opinion", but an opinion that was transmitted from the Companions. Since both times were held by the principal figures of the Hanafi School, both are valid and so if the congregational prayer is being held according to the earlier time, praying at this time would be permitted. It would in fact be encouraged if that is the only time where you could catch the congregation and forming a second congregation would cause unnecessary fitna in the Umma.

- "The time of maghrib is from that point until the disappearance of the red twilight…" like with Asr, this is disagreed upon between Abu Hanifa and his "Two Companions" (Sahibayn). As the commentator explains, though the author prefers the earlier time, the later time was adopted in much of the world where the Hanafi School was officially sanctioned by the government. It is possible that the author prefers the earlier times as a consequence of his being in Egypt and not desiring to break with the precedent that had already been established by the Malikis and Shafi`is before the Hanafis arrived there - hence his reference to it being the "fatwa" position. The difference between the "red" and "white" position is similar to the difference we mentioned about Fajr above. However, with Isha there is the added complication that the Shafi`is interpret "redness" slightly differently than the Malikis and the Sahibayn[2]. The Shafi`i interpretation of "red" results in a slightly earlier time. So though the earlier "opinion" is not common outside of the Middle-East, please be aware that there are actually three different times that are argued for the beginning of Isha. As with everything else, we encourage you to follow what the Ummah inside the prison has agreed upon as long as it is valid and changing or adding an additional congregation would cause unnecessary fitna. Most calendars are according to either the 15 or 18 degree determination and both of these are valid Hanafi opinions.

- In terms of the prayer calendars, out of all of the prayer times, Maghrib is the most dependent upon the atmosphere. While the sun may be below the level of the horizon theoretically, humidity, ozone density, temperature and pressure all refract the sun's light in ways that a mathematical calculation cannot take into consideration. So there is a theoretical sunset that is posted in newspapers/printed on calendars and an actual sunset that can only be observed with the naked eye. Maghrib is established according to the actual

---

[2] Due to their central role in the Hanafi School, Imam Muhammad al-Shaybani and Qadi Abu Yusuf are referred to as the "Two Companions" or "Sahibayn". In order to get you use to that term, which you will find frequently referenced in Hanafi legal works, we will start using it from now on when referring to them.

sunset, not the theoretical one. As a result, I have witnessed myself the posted time for Maghrib be up to 6 minutes too early at the worst, but more often around 2 or 3 minutes too early depending on the time of year. Anyone who broke their fast immediately (i.e., to the second) according to a calendar that did not take this calculation problem into consideration (as most of them do not) has likely broken their fast too early. However, we do not assume that this has happened unless we know for sure that is the case. In the future, you should wait at least a few minutes after the posted time of Maghrib to break your fast and pray. I myself have adopted a practice of waiting an additional 7 minutes before breaking my fast or praying Maghrib in order to remove my personal doubts. Unfortunately, I have been accused of "going against the Sunna" for doing so since others claimed that I was "delaying breaking of the fast". However, we have to understand that "delaying" the fast means intentionally waiting to break one's fast until well after the sun has set. It is not a "delay" if you are waiting to ensure the sun has indeed set out of precaution, especially given the fact that the prayer times are not established through calculation, but observation. Far too many people do not adequately understand the Qur'an and Sunna and you will find as you increase in your understanding that people blame you for doing things that go against their particular understanding which is frequently inadequate or outright incorrect. Therefore, with issues like this that can potentially cause people to accuse you of starting fitna, we recommend you quietly do what you know is correct without challenging, correcting or even declaring what you are doing to others. You should also not tell people that their prayer or fast is invalid unless you have confirmed that the timing for that day is wrong, but you also have a personal obligation to have certainty before either your fast is broken or your prayer is performed. There is no taqlid to lifeless pieces of paper that have no religious authority. The only thing we can trust in this regard is the public call of a trained mu`adhdhin whose job it is to physically sight the times of the prayer and inform the community based upon his expertise. Given that Shaykh Rami and myself have both noticed frequently that the posted time for Maghrib is too early, we recommend the above practice be adopted by our students, while not making it a public issue or doubting the validity of anyone else's fasts or prayers.

"The following times are recommended…"

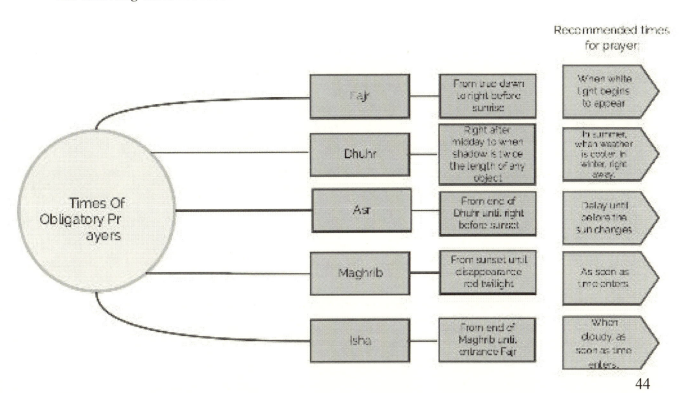

- Any time between the beginning of a prayer's time and its end is permissible to pray in. Generally speaking, it is preferred to pray at the beginning of the time, except for the circumstances mentioned by the author. For some reason, many Muslims believe that it is unlawful to delay the prayer within this time, but that is not the case. As long as the prayer is performed between the two times indicated in the text, no sin has occurred and there is no blame on the individual or community. Therefore, if the prayer is delayed a bit in order to ensure that more people can attend, no one should make an issue out of it. It is actually recommended to delay Fajr and Asr year round in the Hanafi School. Likewise with Dhuhr in the Maliki School. Anyone who claims that it is unlawful or makruh to delay the prayer a few moments or even an hour or more (when the day is long enough to permit this) is in fact declaring something that is permissible to be impermissible. They need to show their proof that this is the case. Quite to the contrary, there are actually several hadith which prove that certain prayers should be delayed a bit and so anyone who claims that praying the prayer within its permissible time is sinful or haram needs to bring their evidence. Otherwise, they are inventing legal rulings and lying about the religion of Allah. However, once the time begins approaching the next prayer, then delay becomes disliked. The prayer should be of primary importance and though it can be "delayed" legitimately, we should not fit the prayer around our schedule, but fit our schedules around the prayer.

"There are three times of the day in which any prayer that was obligatory before…"
- *I.e.*, if the prayer occurs during any of these three times, it is batil. Most of these are well-known, however sunrise is a problem. If you are praying Fajr and the sun hits the horizon in the midst of your prayer, it has been invalidated and must be made up as a make-up prayer after the sun is no longer touching the horizon. So while Fajr should be delayed a bit until the morning is a bit brighter (*i.e.*, faces can be distinguished without artificial light), it should not be delayed so excessively that you risk invalidating the prayer due to sunrise.

"It is disliked to pray voluntary prayers in the following times…"
- "During a religious sermon…" *i.e.*, it is disliked to perform any prayer while a sermon is being delivered or when the imam stands before the congregation during Jumu`ah, as the commentator explains. As for the hadith which seems to suggest otherwise, in longer narrations, the Prophet (Allah bless him and give him peace) stopped giving his sermon while the Companion he ordered to pray two raka'as was performing his nafl. For this reason, many scholars considered this to be an exceptional circumstance and not a sunna or proof that praying while the imam is delivering the khutba is permissible. Quite to the contrary, the Prophet (Allah bless him and give him peace) forbade people to even tell their neighbor to hush if they are talking, which is unlawful for them to do and therefore would ordinarily be obligatory to correct. Therefore, if something that is ordinarily obligatory becomes unlawful during the Friday sermon, something that is only generally recommended is even more clearly impermissible to do. However, this is a difference of opinion and neither those who refuse to pray while the imam is delivering the khutba nor those who believe it permissible to pray tahiyat al-masjid while the khutba is going on should be blamed or criticized for their chosen position.

FIQH 112: RITUAL PRAYER (SALAT)

Disliked Times for Nafl Prayer

- Just prior to the three times when prayer is invalid
- During a religious sermon
- Prior to Subh (excluding the Raka`atyn al-Fajr)
- After Subh until sunrise
- After Asr until sunset

THE CALL TO PRAYER AND ITS COMMENCEMENT

- The adhan and iqama are famously said the same way in the Hanafi School. There are actually three sound wordings of the adhan and three sound wordings of the iqama. No one who calls any of them according to the sound transmissions should be blamed or criticized, nor should anyone be forced to call the adhan or iqama a certain way since all three wordings preferred by the Four Canonical Schools are all valid. In fact, many scholars recommended that in places where there is a mix of people, the adhan and iqama's call be rotated so that the people get used to hearing the adhan and iqama said different ways and do not therefore mistakenly believe that only one way to call either of them is valid.

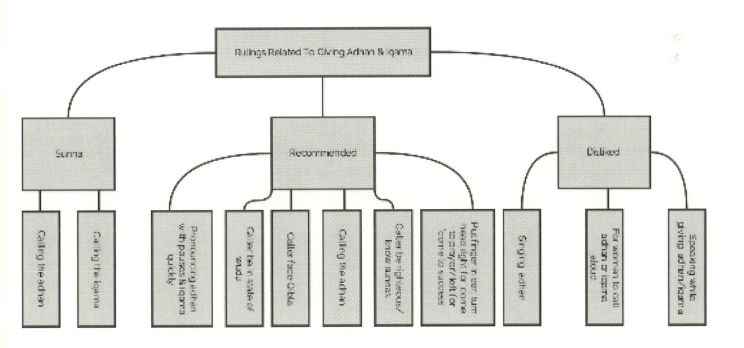

Rulings Related To Giving Adhan & Iqama

- **Sunna**
  - Calling the adhan
  - Calling the iqama
- **Recommended**
  - Pronouncing adhan with pauses & iqama quickly
  - Caller be in state of wudu
  - Caller face Qibla
  - Calling the adhan
  - Caller being right/even/knows sunna
  - Put finger in ear, turn head right for 'come to prayer' left for 'come to success'
- **Disliked**
  - Singing adhan
  - For a woman to call adhan or iqama
  - Speaking while giving adhan/iqama

FIQH 112: RITUAL PRAYER (SALAT)

CONDITIONS OF THE PRAYER

- As should have been clear from FIQH 111, the difference between conditions (shurut) and integrals (arkan) is that the conditions are external states that should be in place prior to the prayer, while the integrals are the major components of the prayer that have to be performing within the prayer. Both must be present in order for the prayer to be valid.

"It is not valid to begin the prayer without having fulfilled its conditions…"
- "Being free from any physical filth, on… and place of prayer…" *i.e.*, the actual points of contact between your hands, feet, forehead and clothing. If there is physical filth around you or near you, but it is not touching you (even if an inch away), the prayer is valid. And as we said, physical filth must be proven by sight or smell and cannot be assumed.
- "Facing the qibla…" has perhaps the widest leeway in the Hanafi School. As long as the qibla is no more than 45 degrees from where you are facing, the prayer is valid. That is the case even if you are intentionally turned away from the qibla, which may be necessary due to spatial considerations.
- "The entrance of the prayer time…" as the commentator states, if there is any doubt about the time having entered and you pray anyway, your prayer is invalid, even if you discover that you had in fact prayed it after it had entered. For this reason, it is better to delay the performance of the prayer for a few minutes than to rush it, especially if you are relying on a calendar since they are frequently off by a few minutes. If you pray at the time according to a calendar without visually confirming yourself, you are actually praying without certainty that the time has come it. As we said above, in the Muslim World, mu`adhdhins typically wait to call the adhan for a few minutes after they believe the time has entered in order to be absolutely sure and not have the sin of other people's invalid prayer upon their neck. As we said, there is no sin for "delaying" the prayer if it is kept within its proper time, only for praying it when its time is about to end or completely outside of its time.
- "The intention…" as we said in relation to the previous chapter, the matter of the niyya is straightforward. And contrary to popular opinion, it is not recommended to state the opinion aloud in the Hanafi School.
- "The tahrima, the place of which is the tongue…" *i.e.*, it is not valid to recite the takbirat al-ihram in one's head as many people unfortunately do. It should be said softly, but loud enough for you to hear yourself. People who stand to pray, raise their hands and do not make a sound have not performed a valid prayer by the consensus of the scholars. The same applies to reciting the Fatiha. In Arabic "recite" means at the very least to move your mouth and tongue. Saying something "in your head" is not included in the meaning of "recite" in the Arabic Language. Anyone who prays without opening their mouth and moving their tongue has not prayed according to any of the Four Canonical Schools, their obligation of those prayers have not been discharged, and each of those prayers must be made up before they die.

"Some of the above conditions are overlooked if there is a valid excuse…"
- *I.e.*, in other words, as the Malikis say, with regard to being free from physical impurities (khabath), covering one's nakedness and facing the Qibla "are conditional upon knowledge and ability". If one is not aware of where the Qibla is or you were unable to face it, that there was impurity on your body or you were unable to remove it, or you were unable to cover your nakedness or were unaware that it was

exposed, the obligation of doing so is lifted. This does not apply to any of the other conditions however, particularly being free from ritual purity (hadath). Being free from hadath is an absolute obligation. Tayammum was legislated for situations where water cannot be found and so there is no excuse for anyone to be ritually impure. Likewise, if you assumed that you were ritually pure, but did not remember that you had accidentally prayed in a state of impurity until after you had completed the prayer, it is retroactively invalid and must be repeated. This is the case even if you did not remember until 20 years later. Once you remember that you were not in a state of ritual purity, the prayer becomes invalidated and must be performed. As for the rare case when you are unable to even make tayammum, due to the lack of any appropriate tayammum material or being physically restrained, then you have to go through the motions of the prayer without technically performing it as a valid prayer as a demonstration to Allah Most High that you would have performed the prayer if you were able to do so in a legally valid way.

INTEGRALS OF THE PRAYER

- "The tahrima according to Imam Muhammad…" *i.e.*, the takbirat al-ihram. Whether or not it is an integral or precondition is merely a matter of semantics. At the end of the day, both categories are required for the prayer to be valid.
- "Standing if one is physically able…" according to the commentator (and what we have been taught by our teachers), if one is unable to stand, the remaining integrals are not left. That is to say, only the obligation of standing is lifted when one is unable to stand. According to the principles of the prayer, if someone who is unable to pray standing sits in a chair and motions the prostration without their head and hands actually touching the ground, the prayer is invalid. The correct way to pray in this situation is to sit on the floor and prostate, as is obligatory upon them, whether that sitting be erect on their knees, in the normal sitting position of the prayer, or "Indian-style". If they can perform the prostration, but would be unable to get up off the floor without extreme difficulty, then it is the obligation of standing that is dropped, not the obligation of prostration. The obligation of prostration would only be dropped for someone who is unable to prostrate outright, due to a back injury for example. Then, and only then, would they be permitted to sit in a chair for the prayer. In that situation, they should stand for the takbirat al-ihram and as much as they can for the Fatiha in the first raka'a as they are able. After this point, they have fulfilled the obligation of standing in their situation and it would be recommended for them to sit for the remainder of the prayer, since standing for the entire duration of any prayer would be considered a hardship for someone who already struggles in the positions of the prayer. In both of these situations, sitting on the ground is superior to sitting on a chair, though sitting in a chair would be permitted for the one who is physically unable to prostrate.
- In the event that someone is unable to stand or sit (either because they are violently ill or the prison is on emergency lockdown and you are being forced to lie on the ground until order has been restored), you have to perform the prayer with head movements, bending your neck for ruku, then bending it further in place of sujud. If you are so ill that you cannot even do this, then you have to make up the prayer when you are able to perform it properly. This includes if you are unable to make either wudu or tayammum before the time ends. However, in the case of someone being ill, if this condition continues for more than 5 prayers, they no longer have to be made up. But this latter consideration does not apply to when you are unable to purify yourself. If you cannot make wudu or tayammum, you still "perform" the prayer without

an intention of prayer and without reciting the Fatiha by going through the motions and adhkar of the prayer as a way of showing Allah Most High that you would have performed it had you been given the opportunity. Once you are able to purify yourself, the prayers are required to be made up, even if this situation lasted for an entire year.

- "Recitation of Qur'an..." as the commentator states, standing while reciting is obligatory. So technically, the obligations of standing apply to the takbirat al-ihram at the beginning and the recitation of the Fatiha in the first two raka'as. As for not reciting behind the imam, doing so is prohibited. However, if someone has difficulty concentrating, there is nothing preventing them from reciting the Fatiha "in their head" without moving their lips in order to aid their concentration and khushu☐.

"It is mandatory that this action be saying the word "al-salam" twice..."

- Unlike the Maliki and Shafi`i Schools, saying both salams is obligatory in the Hanafi School, but not fard. However, if a Hanafi is following behind someone who follows a different school, the validity of their prayer as a follower is based the certainty of the imam that his own prayer is valid. Thus, as long as the imam is following a valid opinion from one of the Four Canonical Schools, one should not suspect the validity of their prayer as a follower if the imam happens to do things that would render his own prayer deficient.

- Also, since saying "al-salam" twice is wajib, technically, the prayer is valid if you only say "Salamu Alaykum" and omit the definitive article, yet it would be deficient. Unfortunately, many people have a habit of only saying "Salamu Alaykum" when ending the prayer, which invalidates it in some of the Schools. Therefore, you should ensure that you pronounce the definite article and some of the scholars (i.e., in West and North Africa) recommend that it be exaggerated a bit in order to ensure that is pronounced. *I.e.*, you would say "Assss-salamu alaykum wa rahmatullahi wa barakatuh". This is not a bad practice to implement.

MANDATORY REQUISITES OF THE PRAYER

"Among them are the following..."

- "To recite the Fatiha..." as we said above means at the very least that their lips and tongue are moved in the "silent" prayers and one's vocal chords vibrate so that you can, at minimum, hear yourself in the prayers said aloud.

EMPHASIZED SUNNAS OF THE PRAYER

"Among them are the following..."

- Recall that intentionally neglecting an emphasized sunna (sunna mu'akkada) is sinful in the Hanafi School. Therefore, neglecting the emphasized sunnas does not affect the validity of the prayer, but doing so repeatedly is sinful.

FIQH 112: RITUAL PRAYER (SALAT)

- "For the man, to place the right hand over the left…" the issue of hand placement is unfortunately given far too much attention in modern times. All of the three positions (below the navel, above the navel and at the sides) are valid positions. However, the Hanafi School is unique in considered hand placement to be a confirmed sunna, while the other Schools consider it to be merely recommended. That being the case, placing the hands anywhere other than below the navel without legitimate reason would be sinful. As for the evidence, all of the ahadith which indicate where the hands should be placed are weak. But the narrations which demonstrate that they should be placed below the navel are actually the strongest. So those who criticize the Hanafi School for following weak reports in this issue are actually themselves following even weaker reports, though very few people realize this. Likewise, the fact that there are slight differences between the prayer of men and women is something that is agreed upon by the scholars.
- "To recite the tasbih three times…" in the Hanafi School is preferred to du'a or any other dhikr since it is demonstrated from the Prophet's usual norm of prayer to do so. The other dhikrs and du'a that are narrated from him (Allah bless him and give him peace) are interpreted to be from things that he said during his nawafil prayers. Thus any du'as that you wish to recite should be left until after the final tashahhud or said during the prostrations of nafl prayers.

ETIQUETTE OF THE PRAYER

- The text and commentary here should be straightforward.

SUPPLICATIONS OF THE PRAYER

"The qunut of the witr prayer…"
- The qunut is a supplication that is only said during witr in the Hanafi School. It is not said during subh as in the Maliki and Shafi`i Schools. And it is wajib and so if it is left, the prayer is valid, but deficient. If one has not memorized any of the narrated supplications of qunut, you can simply say "Ya Rubb" or "Allahumma ighfirli" three times or "Allahuma ighfirli, wa-hdini, wa-rhamni, wa-`aafini, wa-rzuqni" and salawat upon the Prophet (*e.g.*, "Allahumma salli ala sayyidina Muhammadin wa aalihi wa sahbihi wa salam.") or any other substantial du'a in Arabic until you have memorized the du'a found on page 192.

THINGS THAT INVALIDATE THE PRAYER

"The following things invalidate the ritual prayer…"
- "To utter a word, even if out of forgetfulness…" *i.e.*, any recognizable sound that is like speech which communicates a message to someone who is not praying is considered "speech" and it invalidates the prayer. This may seem odd at first, but remember that in Arabic, "sounds" like "bi" "fi" are actually proper words on their own and therefore is considered to be speech. In order to ensure the validity of your prayer, avoid making any sounds unnecessarily.

- "To respond to someone's statement…" if you are trying to indicate to someone that you are praying, instead of making dhikr external to the prayer or reciting a verse of the Qur'an (which would be considered speech due to your intention), you should instead recite aloud what you were reciting silently or raise your voice a little more than usual when saying the things aloud that should be said aloud (*e.g.*, takbirs and tasmiya☐). That way, you are not actually speaking to them, but merely allowing them to understand that you are in the midst of prayer without actually violating its sanctity.
- "To turn one's torso away…" *i.e.*, turning one's head away does not break the prayer, but is makruh without reason. So the Shi`a, for instance, who say that the head should not be turned when giving the salams because it allegedly breaks the prayer are incorrect in their reasoning. What breaks the prayer is turning one's entire body away from the Qibla and turning one's head during the concluding salams does not. Furthermore, it is proven from the ahadith that doing so is recommended.
- "To carry an unexcused amount of filth…" *i.e.*, it is either in your pockets or attached to your clothing. If you were praying besides someone who was wearing a pig skin jacket (for instance), this would not invalidate your prayer since you are not carrying his jacket, even though it is touching you. The only time someone else's impurity would invalidate your prayer would be if some of it transferred over to your clothing. So if someone had an uncontrollable emission of urine and it got on your clothing, your prayer would be invalidated if it was more than a dirham. If they had a pig skin jacket which had gotten wet, there is no problem since nothing would transfer onto your person.
- "For one's nakedness to be uncovered…" *i.e.*, if a sister's hijab partially slipped off, but she fixed it immediately, it would be excused. What is more of an issue though, is the lower back of men. Because Western shirts barely go beyond our waist, if you are not wearing suspenders, an overcoat or a t-shirt properly tucked in, men frequently have their lower backs inadvertently exposed when they go into prostration. This technically invalidates the prayer, so we should take care to either wear a loose jacket when we pray or make sure that either our t-shirt or actual shirt is tucked into our pants. Unfortunately, many (if not most) men make this mistake and far too many of us will find that on the Day of Judgment, we do not have as many prayers in our account as we otherwise thought we did.

THINGS THAT ARE DISLIKED IN THE PRAYER

- "To roll up one's sleeves" is taken by some people to mean that rolling up one's clothing is disliked in the prayer, however other works clarify that what is intended by this is someone to either do so sloppily or to do so in order to avoid them touching the ground. If one's sleeves are so long that they would prevent you from directly touching the ground with your hands, folding them over the a few times in order to expose your palms is not disliked - as the commentator explains.[3] The same applies to one's pant legs. Having them below the ankles is mildly disliked (makruh tanzihan) or merely against what is preferred (khilaf al-awla) and only sinful if done out of arrogance.[4] However, this is completely unconnected to the prayer.

---

[3] NOTE: It is mentioned that Ali ibn Abi Talib used to like to wear his sleeves so that they covered most of his hands. If someone has their sleeves like this, rolling them up a few times in order for the hands to directly touch the ground is permitted and not disliked.

[4] It could be argued that this latter is not particularly relevant for Americans since the Arabs at the time of the revelation trailed their garments out of pride as a way of showing that they could afford to get their clothing dirty.

People folding up their pant legs for the prayer and unrolling them afterwards are potentially committing an act of innovation since the disliked nature of having the pants below the ankle is a ruling that applies <u>to men</u> in general and has nothing to do with the prayer. The hadith "Allah does not accept the prayer of a man who drags his lower garment" is not proof against this claim, as the Prophet did not say "in the prayer" but merely "a man who drags his lower garment". Having the pants below the ankle is not an invalidator of the prayer, but having arrogance in your heart is an invalidator of residency in Paradise. But it is more precautionary to wear one's pants at or above the ankle so that they do not drag on the ground, since doing so still remains makruh. But if one is unable to do this (because you do not have access to a tailor for instance) and so they neatly roll their pants up in order that they not prevent your heels from touching the ground, this is similar to someone who rolls up their sleeves in order to expose their hands.

- "To gather one's garment close to the body…" for the reason cited above. This was done in order to keep them from touching the ground and getting "dirty". Western pants are unfortunately cut in a way that is not necessarily conducive to the positions of the prayer, so if you need to pull up your pants a bit in order that the crotch not be too low and make it uncomfortable for you to sit properly in the tashahhud, this is not what was intended by this ruling. Wa-Llahu alim.
- "To place a shawl on one's head or shoulders…" is actually recommended for the imam in the Maliki School. However, in the Hanafi School, anything that is allowed to freely hand (irsal) is disliked. Part of the wisdom is, perhaps, that it causes an unnecessary distraction and forces you to make movements that are external to the prayer in order to move it out of the way when you are prostrating.
- "To close one's eyes…" as the commentator states, unless you are doing so to help you concentrate. This does not mean for the entire prayer however, but for a moment during the prayer. Another legitimate excuse would be if a woman passed in front of you (or a man who is not properly dressed in the case of women) and you needed to close your eyes in order to keep from inadvertently seeing the haram. The same would apply to anything else that is a distraction.
- "To prostrate on a picture…" *i.e.*, to intentionally prostrate on a rug or carpet (or shirt) which has 2-dimensional images woven into it. To intentionally prostrate to an actual picture out of veneration of the one in the image is unlawful and out of worship is an act of kufr. The former is common in Eastern cultures. It is common for martial artists to prostrate to their sensei for example, as it is for Hindus to prostrate to their elders or to their graves. When they do so, they are not worshipping them, but showing them honor and respect. But this is the reason why the scholars of the Subcontinent make a distinction between a prostration of veneration and prostration of worship since they were both a part of their culture and people who are ignorant in their religion have a tendency to revert back to pre-Islamic customs without realizing they are problematic. Though both types of prostrations are haram, only the latter is considered kufr.
- "To pray in work clothes…" if you have other clothing available. Abu Hanifa was famous for dressing up and adorning himself with perfume as though he was going to meet a dignitary for every prayer he performed in order to honor the prayer as it deserved to be honored.
- "To pray with one's head uncovered…" is considered makruh since it is established from the ahadith that the Prophet (Allah bless him and give him peace) almost always prayed with his head covered. Additionally, walking around bareheaded was considered socially unacceptable in pre-modern Muslim

---

Most Americans who have their pant legs below their ankle only do so because our clothing is mass manufactured and not individually tailored.

cultures. The only men who did were teenagers or "fools". As for the condition of "unless done out of humility", this is an exception to the general rule. No one removes their kufi or turban out of humility in our times. Rather, they are both worn out of humility or compliance with the custom of the Prophet, his Companions and the Muslims as a whole. The idea that uncovering the head specifically is more humble is a novel opinion and is only said as a way of undermining the default position of the Hanafi School. As for the ruling itself, though it is makruh to intentionally pray bareheaded, if you are being prevented from wearing it by prison administration, we have confirmed with a classical trained scholar that this is enough to remove the potential sinful nature of doing so. A reasonable compromise that they should not have an issue with is to allow a white kufi to be worn during the prayer, Qur'anic study and taleem, but kept in one's pocket during all other times if they have a policy against group affiliations that do not exclude religion.

- "To pray when food has been served" means that when it would be a distraction, as the commentator clarifies. If it is a distraction, it would be permissible to delay eating until one was satiated, as long as doing so would not enter one into the makruh time of the prayer or miss it entirely. However, with respect to Maghrib, since the time is short, you should break your fast with enough food and water to stave off your hunger, pray and then have your proper meal. This ruling does not mean you spend an hour eating, drinking tea and chatting with family and then pray Maghrib when it is convenient for you while using this ruling as an excuse.

- "To pray in the presence of a picture…" applies to drawings. There are some Hanafi Scholars who exclude photographs from "pictures" which originally applied to statues or hand-drawn images. Therefore, if you are in a room which has photographs and you are unable to remove them, then you should get permission to cover them with a sheet. If you are unable to do that, then you can follow this ruling, while trying your best not to directly face the photographs.

- "To pray near filth" meaning the legally determined filth that has been mentioned in the previous chapter. Filth is not assumed where it has not been visually confirmed or known to be frequent in a particular place (such as in a lavatory). As such, we do not assume that any floor is filthy and unsuited for prayer unless it is the floor of a bathroom or isolation cell where people are known to urinate or defecate in protest of their increased level of confinement. There is nothing wrong with cleaning the floor of your cell, but we do not assume that the prayer is invalid due to the existence of filth due to the mere assumption that filth is present without any evidence.

- "To pray in a congregation while standing alone…" should not be done unless you can pull someone to stand with you. However, this should not be done in a way that creates a future gap in the previous line. Also, pulling someone out of their line to join with you is disagreed upon in some schools. So while the commentator mentions that it should not be done when people are ignorant of the ruling, the fact that this is not agreed upon is. Some of the schools consider praying by oneself in a line to only be an issue if you are doing it intentionally to separate yourself. So unless you know that someone is aware of this ruling or it is very likely that someone will join you, you should follow the fatwa and pray by oneself in a new line.

THINGS THAT ARE PERMISSIBLE IN THE PRAYER

"It is recommended for one to place a barrier in front of him…"
- Using a sutra is only recommended and not obligatory or a condition of the prayer. Furthermore, as the commentator mentions, not using a sutra is only makruh when you are praying in an area where it is expected that someone may pass in front of you. This also means that if someone does not have a sutra and you are able to walk around them, you should walk around them. If you have to walk in front of them due to their blocking the walkway and you cannot wait, you should walk in front of them beyond the point where they would prostrate with their head on the floor if you are able. Anything beyond this point is not considered to be "in front" of them for the purpose of the prayer. "In front of" a praying person means directly in front of them such that they can touch you with their arm, as the Prophet indicated should be done if someone tries to walk in front of you while praying. If you are beyond their reach, then you are not "in front" of them by the Prophetic definition. If you cannot walk past the point of their prostration, you can walk in front of them and the sin is upon them for blocking the only exit.

"The following things in the ritual prayer are not disliked…"
- "To kill a snake or scorpion…" or any other thing in which you actively fear for your safety, such as a feral dog or another human being. Breaking the prayer out of fear in this case would be permissible. If there is an active threat against your life or person, then you should ensure that you pray in a way in which you can ensure your own safety; *i.e.*, with your back against the wall or in an area where the individual who seeks to harm you has no access. However, studies have shown that people often exaggerate the threats against us in our own mind and so we should not use unreasonable fear as an excuse to leave certain obligatory aspects of the prayer, but instead take the necessary precautions for us to pray in a legally valid way while maintaining our safety.

"It is acceptable for one to pray on carpets or rugs..."
- This is said perhaps because someone could reason that since it invalidates the prayer to prostrate on something that raises one's forehead a certain amount off the ground, praying on a thick carpet or a rug would be problematic or disliked at the very least. That is not the case in the Hanafi School. That being said, as the commentator states, it is preferable to pray directly on the ground. The opposite being the case is not true however and many Muslims seem to believe that it is recommended or even obligatory to pray on a prayer rug. This is not established in the works of fiqh. It is only permissible to pray on a rug and would be raised to a level of recommendation if it is needed in order to counteract an rough, hot or cold terrain or obligatory when praying directly on either of the former would be harmful or when it is placed over a <u>dry</u> impurity when no other spot is available. So while the Shi`a, who insist that the prayer is only

valid if prayed directly on the earth or what grows from it are not correct in declaring the prayer to be invalid, they are not entirely wrong in their concern either.

BREAKING THE PRAYER

"It is permissible to break the ritual prayer if one is being robbed, even if it belongs to someone else…"
- It is permissible to break for someone else since we are people who enjoin the good and forbid the evil and theft is clearly something which should be prevented if one is capable of doing so. Someone may ask, "Why is property more important than the prayer?" It is not, however, protection of property is one of the main objectives (maqasid) of the Shari`a and being without one's property can be objectively harmful. In the situation where the prayer needs to be broken due to potential theft, the sin of doing so would be upon the thief.

"It is mandatory… for... a blind person…"
- Likewise a small child who is not aware of the dangers of his surroundings or a deaf person in a similar situation as the blind. The same also applies to supererogatory (nafl) prayers if one's mother or father are calling you and would be angered by your lack of a response. This latter applies to no one else though. However, it does not extend to the obligatory prayers, unless you understand from their tone that they are in danger in which case the danger would be the reason for breaking the prayer and not their potential anger.

"A midwife may delay her ritual prayer…"
- Midwives were the doctors of the time and so the same would apply to a surgeon who is actively engaged in trying to save someone's life and their stopping their work to perform the prayer would risk the life of their patient. If they are unable to find a substitute who can cover for them while they tend to their prayer, the preservation of life comes first and they make up their prayer after this has been accomplished. They cannot pray while they perform surgery since it has already been established that excessive movement renders the prayer null and void.

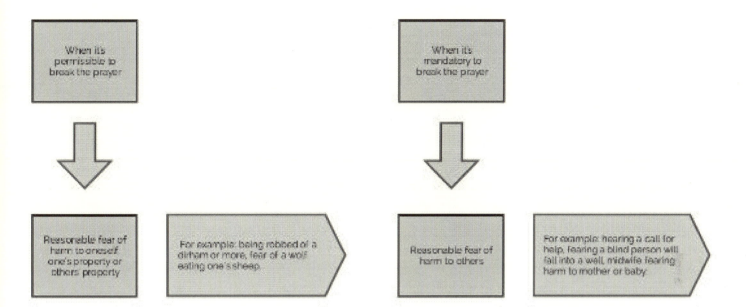

ABANDONING THE PRAYER

- What is mentioned in this section is only permissible for the legal authority in an Islamic country. For that reason, we shall not get into the details or discuss the differences of opinion which may exist over what is said here. The only thing that we take from this discussion is the seriousness with which missing a single prayer was taken by the scholars of the past. As for implementation of its rulings, it is not permissible for civilians of Muslim lands to take into their own hands or Muslims in non-Muslim lands to implement discretionary punishments (ta`zir) without the permission of the government - which is not something that has been granted to Muslims in the United States. The most that we can do is exert social pressure, but this must be done with wisdom in a way that does not make the situation worse. Isolating, shunning or excommunicating people because of sins that they do in our times and in our situation, in most cases is a guaranteed way of pushing our brothers and sisters into the arms of the Disbelievers who are more than happen to accept them the way that they currently are. This will prove more destructive to their faith than remaining in their company and tolerating the way that they are as long as they do not commit sins in your presence. Our time is not a time is isolating, but keeping people's company and trying to motivate them towards the good with gentleness and mercy. Though Imam al-Akhdari says in the beginning of his work "It is not permissible to befriend a transgressor (fāsiq) nor to sit with him, unless there is a necessity." This only applies in a Muslim land when others isolating them would be a strong motivation for their repentance. In non-Muslim lands or in Muslim lands where corruption and immorality is widespread, we way of the scholars is to benefit people by their presence as long as sins are not openly committed and doing so would not be detrimental to the person who is trying to inspire tawba. As the Prophet (Allah bless him and give him peace) said, "Shaytan is with the one who is alone" (Tirmidhi) and "Do not help Shaytan against your brother."[5] (Bukhari)

PRAYING ON A RIDING ANIMAL

"Obligatory and mandatory prayers are invalid if performed on a riding animal…"
- For the reasons we alluded to above: you cannot ensure that the obligations of the prayer are upheld. In the case of the riding animal, firstly due to your being unable to face the Qibla properly, as well as stand and prostrate on the ground. However, if you are being transported and you will be unable to pray standing before the time of the prayer ends, the necessity is established since you would not be permitted to stand on the bus due to the security protocols of the prison officials.

"If one prays in a ship…"
- This implies that it is valid to pray on a ship, even though it is not technically connected to the ground. The same applies to prayer on a plane in the Hanafi School according to the fatwa of many contemporary scholars. Even though the plane is not touching the ground, the floor of the plane would take the place of the earth since it is firm. There is no issue for either cause.

PRAYER OF THE TRAVELLER

"The minimum period of travel whereby certain legal rulings take effect is three days…"
- Or approximately 50 American miles or 77 or 78 kilometers as the commentator mentions. Arabic miles and British miles are equivalent, while American miles are slightly shorter. But as the commentator says, these are just estimations. You do not have to be 100% exact. Also know that there is a difference of opinion on this matter, so followers for other Schools may have different lengths. The Shafi`is and Hanbalis aren't too much different, but the Malikis have a much shorter distance. Keep this in mind if you are travelling with a group. Everyone is obliged to follow their own School and differences like these should not be made an issue of.
- Among those legal rulings which take effect are forgoing fasting during Ramadan. However, this is only permissible if one was outside one's city limits prior to Fajr entering (as the commentator also mentions). This means that if you begin a trip at 11 am, you are not permitted to break your fast due to travel. Only the person who is a traveller at the time the fast entered is permitted to break the fast. If you were a resident at the time Fajr entered, you were not a traveller and so that rukhsa does not apply to you. You

---

[5] Though the latter was said in response to a Companion who cursed a man who was repeatedly punished for public drunkenness, it is a principle by which we interact with each other. We do not compromise on our religious principles, but we also do not push people into the arms of disobedience and disbelief through our rash, unsympathetic decisions when there is hope that people can be improved by our company.

cannot retroactively consider yourself to be a traveller. The overwhelming majority of scholars agree on this point, irrespective of the particular Madhhab they follow.[6]

"Once he reaches a city or village and intends on staying there for fifteen days..."

- One is legally a "traveller" in the Hanafi School once you leave your city of "residence" and do not remain in the same place for at least 15 full days. If you are setting out for travel and are still in your city or you have remained at a single destination for 15 days, you are no longer considered a traveller. Instead, you are a legal resident. From this, we understand that one being a "resident" is a legal designation that has nothing to do with your "legal residence" from a secular standpoint or the city that you consider to be your home. Our "home" is Paradise - in sha Allah - and until we reach there, nothing is permanent.
  <u>NOTE</u>: This is a place where the Hanafis have a different opinion than the other three Schools. Without going into unnecessary detail, they generally consider the time period to be 5 days or 20 prayers. As we said above, in the event that you are travelling with a group of people who do not all follow the same school, every individual is obliged to follow their own School without being blamed or pressured to act contrary to what is established. So it will happen frequently that you will pray a shortened prayer while others in your party are praying as residents and that is okay.

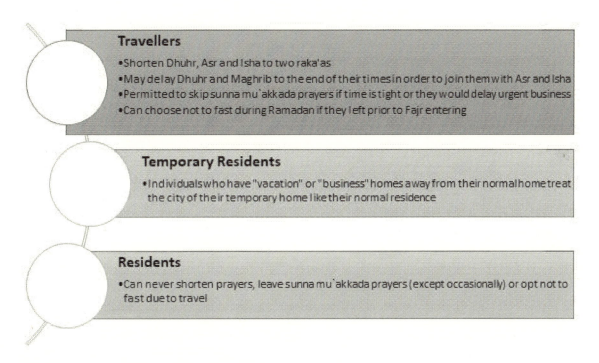

"The journey ends upon entering his normal place of residence..."

---

[6] Since fasting Ramadan is obligatory, whenever you read "break the fast" in works of fiqh, it can either mean stopping your fast during the middle of the day (*e.g.*, as a result of severe illness) or not fasting the upcoming day when doing so is permissible (*e.g.*, a traveller). So when the traveller "breaks his fast" it means that he has made the decision during the night not to fast the upcoming day. It does not mean that he has decided to travel the next day and so he can break his fast once he begins his journey, even if he left at noon. If he did not begin his journey before Subh entered, he was a resident when the fast entered and residents are obliged to fast unless they are one of those people for whom the obligation to fast is lifted.

- *I.e.*, even if you don't intend on staying there for 15 days, you are no longer considered a traveller once you re-enter your "normal" city limits. If someone has two homes, such as a truck driver or sailor who may have a second home set up where he rests in between trips, this second home takes the same ruling as his "normal" place of residence if he has stayed there 15 days at least once in the past. There are some scholars who extend this to your parental (*i.e.*, the home you grew up in if your parents still live there), but the stronger opinion is that this is only considered to be the case if you actually still consider this place to be "your" home.[7] In the case of your incarceration, whether or not you consider the institutions your permanent residence, if you remain there for 15 complete days, you pray as a resident and not a traveller. The status of "traveller" or "resident" does not depend on your intention. The only thing that is considered is the amount of time you remain in any particular city.

"If he prays behind a resident…"
- He must pray a full four raka's. It is not valid in the Hanafi School (or any other school we are aware of) for a traveller to pray two raka's behind a resident imam who is praying four raka's. Whoever does this, their prayer is invalid prayer and it must be repeated. This includes if they did so in the past, though you will not be considered sinful if you were not aware that this was not valid. If you are travelling and desire to maintain your travel prayer, you should either pray on your own or pray in the Masjid after or before the official congregational time in a way that does not cause fitna (providing that the Masjid allows congregations outside of the official one).

"In the opposite scenario, the prayer would be valid…"
- The author is a little unclear, but the commentator should have cleared this up. To summarize, what the Imam means is that since it is wajib for a traveller to shorten the prayer, if a traveller leads the prayer and mistakenly prays as a resident, the prayer of a resident behind him is invalid for the reasons mentioned in the text and commentary on page 92. However, this is provided that the imam is Hanafi (which the author and commentator have assumed since it is a Hanafi text). If the imam is Maliki or Shafi`i, their shortening the prayer is not obligatory and therefore the prayer behind them should be considered valid unconditionally.

"A missed prayer on a journey is made up…"
- What this implies is that all prayers must be made up when they are missed. The opinion that a missed prayer is kufr and does not need to be made up is a weak opinion overall and not valid in the Hanafi School, period. The opinion that they cannot be made up and that you therefore should not try and should pray nawafil instead is aberrant.

"A traveller in a permissible journey and one of disobedience are equivalent…"
- This is only a technical point. It is not a license to commit acts of disobedience or declaration that sin is "no big deal". Rather, even if someone is in a state of disobedience, they are expected to follow the Prophet's Sunna and there is no excuse not to. Similarly, the Hanafis refuse to negate something that the Prophet (Allah bless him and give him peace) permitted due to some external factor not directly tied to

---

[7] For example, when I lived with my mother when she fell ill, I was married and my wife lived in another place. So I considered both my mother's home and my "wife's" home to be my home and would leave off shortening the prayer whenever I entered the city limits of either place.

FIQH 112: RITUAL PRAYER (SALAT)

the original dispensation. In this case, they insist that wiping over khuffs or shortening the prayer are not negated by an external consideration of sinfulness in the intention of the trip. We understand from these two points that the Prophet's Sunna comes before every other consideration.

- Though it is not directly discussed in this section, travel is not a sufficient reason to leave any of the obligations of the prayer unless you have absolutely no control over the circumstances of your travel.[8] Therefore, the mere fact that you are travelling in a vehicle is not enough reason to permit the prayer to be done while seated. Rather, if you must stand and face the Qibla as best you can. If you cannot stand due Department of Prisons transportation rules, the obligation of doing so is not lifted because you are travelling, but because you are being prevented from standing. Therefore, if you can pray before arriving or wait until after and not miss the prayer, you should do so. Otherwise you would be permitted to pray and must do so with as many obligations of the prayer that you are able to uphold.

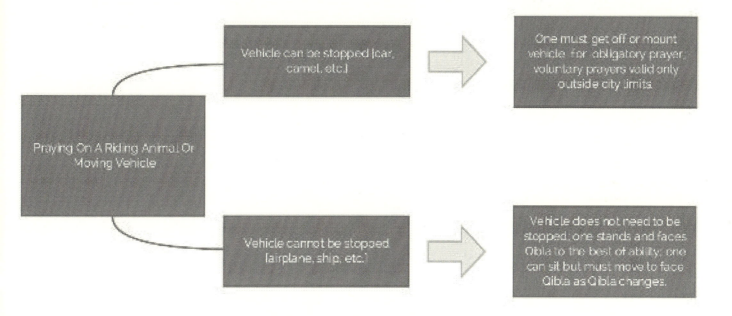

PRAYER OF THE SICK PERSON

"If it is difficult or impossible for a sick person to stand…"
- As we said in previous sections, the fact that one cannot do one obligation does not necessarily mean the others drop away. Whether someone is sick, injured or suffering from the ailments which typically affect the elderly, if they cannot stand, they are still required to bow and prostrate. And as the commentator states, the obligation of standing is so established that it must be done even if you have to lean on a wall or support themselves and even if only for the takbirat al-ihram and first few verses of the Fatiha. From this, we can understand what type of difficulty lifts the obligation of standing. The same would apply to prostration. It can only be left if one is unable to perform it without undue hardship. Otherwise, if any

---

[8] Rather, this can all be inferred from the discussion about facing the Qibla and praying on an animal when the ground is so muddy that it would cause your face to sink into the ground.

portion of the prayer that is obligatory is left unperformed simply because it is considered "inconvenient" or "difficult" without being preventatively so, the entire prayer is invalid. For this reason, many scholars have condemned the presence of chairs in the prayer area, since many people who use them would otherwise figure out how to perform the prayer properly were chairs made available as an "easy" solution. When the Prophet (Allah bless him and give him peace) was sick and on his deathbed, he still got out of bed and prayed sitting besides Abu Bakr whenever he had the strength to do so.

"If sitting is impossible…"

- The important point here is the last thing the commentator says in footnote 324: "[O]ne does not pray by eye or eyebrow movements nor in one's heart (or mind) alone." If you are so ill that you can only move your eyes in the Hanafi School, the obligation of prayer is temporarily lifted until you have recovered. If this state lasts for less than five prayers, they must be made up once you recover. If it last for five or more, you do not have to make it up. The same applies if you fell unconscious or into a coma.

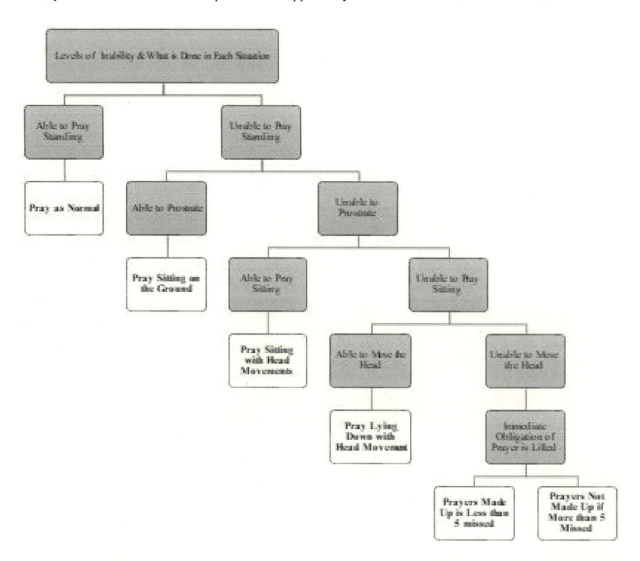

FIQH 112: RITUAL PRAYER (SALAT)

BEING ABSOLVED FROM THE OBLIGATION OF PRAYER OR FASTING

"If a sick person… or a traveller… died before attaining unto alternatives…"
- The text and commentary should be clear. But if we reflect on this, we understand that the only excuse anyone has for not making up prayers or fasts which were obligatory upon them is death before their excuse had resolved itself. The same can be understood from the next paragraph which obligates fidya for prayers in the same way that it is obligatory for missed fasts.

THE WITR PRAYER

"The witr prayer is mandatory…"
- This means that it must be made up if it is missed. However, someone who was not following the Hanafi School and then started following it (as most of you are probably doing now), they are not held accountable for making up witr since the position that they were following in the past was valid. This establishes a general principle that "rukhsa-seeking" is permitted in order to maintain the validity of past acts of worship, but it remains unlawful for the present.

"A group can pray the witr in congregation only in Ramadan…"
- This is based on the principle that acts of worship are not performed in a group without proof that doing so is recommended. However, as the commentator mentions, it is permitted for a small group, such as a husband and wife or members of a household.

THE EMPHASIZED SUNNA PRAYERS

- As the commentator mentions, the fact that they are emphasized sunnas means that they are a step below wajib, but are treated as though they are obligatory. That being so, if one has make-up prayers to perform, the emphasized sunnas are not left unless one would not be able to complete their makeup prayers in a timely fashion.

"Those consisting of two rakas…"
- "Before fajr" is the most emphasized of them all, as the commentator states. This is so established that many of the Companions prayed the two raka'ats of fajr if they arrived late to the congregation, even if the fard prayer was being performed. This includes Ibn Masud and Ibn Umar. Thus, this prayer is excluded from the general rule that "There is no prayer after the iqama" which means that no non-obligatory prayer can be initiated after the iqama for the congregation has been called. If one is praying a sunna which you began prior to the iqama being called, you complete your prayer by the

consensus of the scholars. Opinions to the contrary are novel, oppose the principles of usul and are thus ignored. However, in the case of the two raka'as of fajr, they are an exception which can be prayed as long as one believes that they can catch at least the second raka'at with the imam and the other conditions mentioned by the commentator are fulfilled (which includes having missed both the two raka'as and fajr in their proper times).

"The following are general sunnas…"

- This means that they do not and should not be made up if they are missed. However, performing them was the Prophet's Sunna and so there is a great reward in upholding them. This is particularly the case with the duha prayer which very few people in our time perform. People of the past would not leave their homes until they had performed it and used it to add baraka to the beginning of their day before men left their homes to go to work. As for the "night prayer" this is referring to tahajjud which many people perform in order to catch the merit of the last ten days of Ramadan. It is not a reference to tarawih.
NOTE: This is also why the "night prayer" is included in both the chapter of tahajjud and prayer in Ramadan in works like the *Muwatta* of Imam Malik. And so those who interpret the hadith of tahajjud in order to limit the number of raka'as of tarawih to two are applying ahadith which are speaking about tahajjud to an entirely different prayer.

THE NIGHT VIGIL OF RAMADAN

"The tarawih prayers are [an emphasized] sunna…. They consist of twenty raka's…"

- If they are not performed as 20 raka's, they are not valid in the Hanafi School. We will not bother to get into an exhaustive defense of this position. If someone does not consider the fact that the Companions undeniably prayed 20 raka'as to be enough proof that doing so is at least permissible, there is no other argument that is going to convince them. If you happen to pray behind someone who only performs 8 raka'as or are praying it with your cellmate who only does 8 raka'as, you would have to do the remaining 12 raka'as on your own. Since the validity of witr is only conditioned (time-wise) on it being prayed after `isha, it would be permissible for you to pray 8 raka's and witr in congregation and then complete the remaining 12 raka's of tarawih on your own.

"It is a communal sunna… to recite the entire Qur'an…"

- which means that the actual prayer is sunna mu`akkada and tarawih should be lead by a hafiz who can recite the entire Qur'an during the month. If this is not possible, then what the commentator states would apply. Also note that it is not permissible to read from a mushhaf in the Hanafi School. Doing so invalidates the prayer as it is considered excessive movement, among other things. As for a quick recitation, what is intended here is a recitation so fast that the rules of tajwid are broken and the meaning of the words becomes distorted (as in discussed in ADAB 102). Otherwise, reciting a little faster than normal in order to simultaneously fulfill the sunna of reciting the entire Qur'an in tarawih, while also not making standing for it difficult on the congregation, there is no problem with this.
- Also, because tarawih is an emphasized sunna, someone who still has make-up prayers should not leave it. However, they should pray their make-ups instead of tahajjud later in the night, since tahajjud is only a general sunna and therefore one's obligatory qada' takes precedence.

PRAYING INSIDE THE KA'BA

- As a policy, this is generally not permitted by the current government except for the royal family and whoever they choose to honor with this distinction. No blame should be targeted towards them for this since it can be considered a solution to the practical problem of the number of people who would like to pray inside the Ka'aba if it were ever made generally open to the public. So while this is interesting and good to know in the event you are able to implement it, it is unlikely to happen for most of us.

"If the congregation forms a circle…"
- This is because it is invalid in the Hanafi School for someone to be in front of the imam. When that occurs, only the prayer of the person(s) that is(are) in front of the imam is invalid.

MAKING UP MISSED PRAYERS

"Maintaining the correct order…"
- Meaning that if one has make up prayers, the order of the make ups and the current prayer must be maintained as they would have been performed unless the three conditions mentioned by the author exist.

"Hence, that which one prays, even witr, is invalid, yet suspended."
- To simplify, "suspended" is a category that exists in the Hanafi School that is easier to understand in terms of financial contracts. If a contract contains a corrupting element, the validity of that contract is "suspended" until that corrupting element is corrected.[9] Similarly, the order is obligatory and if prayed out of order, they prayers are corrupted and are automatically suspended. If enough time passes to render the order no longer necessary, the suspension is lifted since the corrupting element is no longer present. Otherwise, in the example mentioned by the commentator, if fajr was made up before the next sunrise, all the prayers done after it was missed are retroactively considered to be nafl and must be repeated with the proper order in place. Continuing with the example that the commentator mentions, if someone misses fajr, does not make it up and prays the remaining prayers of the day, all those prayers are considered to be nafl and not fard. So he would still owe that entire day's prayers. However, if a full day passes and he does not make up that fajr he missed until after sunrise of the next day, those previous day's prayers are now retroactively considered fard and only the missed fajr needs to be made up. This is a rather technical point and establishes the principle. Practically speaking, you should never actually implement this ruling unless you simply forgot that you had missed fajr until an entire day has passed. If you <u>inadvertently</u> slept through fajr, you are not actually considered sinful unless you don't make it up before dhuhr. Once dhuhr enters and you knowingly pray dhuhr without first making up fajr, you are doing something that is haram

---

[9] This is not actually how it is described, but for the sake of explaining the term, it is similar to how it is used in this chapter in fiqh. Technically, the a corrupt contract is just corrupt until it is corrected. "Suspended" is actually not applied in that situation and the scholars simply insist that tawba is obligatory and tawba wound entail that the corrupting element of the contract be corrected. That is why suspended is in quotes.

and your dhuhr is not valid. Your dhuhr only becomes valid if you fail to make up fajr for a full day, whereupon the prayers of the previous day are retroactively considered to be valid. <u>But this entails that you prayed four prayers that you knew were technically invalid and would only become valid if you purposely delayed making up fajr until after the time of the next fajr had expired.</u> If you do not quite understand this, it is okay. Just know that the situation described in footnote 353 is referring to the legal ruling of the situation, but morally, the individual who does this intentionally is sinful and that entire situation could have been averted had he only made up fajr before he prayed dhuhr.

"One who did not immigrate to Muslim lands after his conversion…"

- As the commentator says, this ruling is no longer applicable, at least not for you all. The original ruling mentioned by the author is based on the idea that someone who converted in a non-Muslim land in the past was in isolation and they therefore had no way of learning the rules of prayer and fasting, so his ignorance is excused. However, ignorance is not an excuse when learning is possible and so, generally speaking, no one who reads is excused for their ignorance of basic things like fasting and prayer - excluding certain lesser known rules that have been identified as exceptions by the scholars *(e.g.,* someone who fully stood after forgetting the first tashhahud not returning to it).[10] If you were taught incorrectly, as were many of us were,[11] you are not sinful for making an honest mistake, but the prayers and fasts need to be made up if they were performed in a way that rendered them invalid. The sin of this situation would fall upon the community who failed to establish the communal obligation of having people who can properly teach others their religion.

CATCHING THE CONGREGATIONAL PRAYER

"Prayer in congregation…"

- This and the commentary should be self-explanatory. The only thing that may be an issue is the final condition mentioned by the commentator. If someone came late to the prayer and is in the process of making up the parts of the prayer that they missed behind the imam after the jama`a has ended their prayer, you should not join with them. This creates a conceptual mess in the Hanafi School since the original latecomer is making up the parts of the prayer that they missed and someone who makes them an imam is following someone who is technically still following another individual. It is tantamount to someone making a member of a congregation his imam, while the imam is leading that individual in the prayer. However, this is potentially valid in other Schools, so if someone insists that you join someone who is clearly in the process of making up their prayer (which you can surmise based on where they are standing), you should politely decline their suggestion. If someone joins you in this situation, you should let them know after they are done that you were making up your prayer as a latecomer so they can make the determination on whether or not they need to repeat their prayer.

---

[10] As the commentator mentions in footnote #378, if you are fully erect, you should not return to the sitting position. The reason being that you have left a fard for a wajib. In some of the schools, this actually invalidates the prayer, but the Shafi`is exclude laymen from having their prayer being invalidated since this is a lesser known rule among the masses.

[11] This includes both Sh. Rami and myself who were not taught initially that it was not valid to recite the Fatiha in your head, which is what "silent" means in English. But "recite" in Arabic necessarily implies that the tongue and lips are moved at minimum.

"365. In general, the later-comer of a congregational prayer makes up the rak'a(s) he missed in the following manner…"

- This is perhaps worded a little oddly. To hopefully simplify what our commentator explained, if you arrive late to a congregational prayer, after the imam has completed his prayer and you stand to complete what you missed, you finish your prayer in form by building on what you caught with the imam, but in wording by reciting what you had missed. So, if you caught just the last raka' with the imam, when you stand to complete what you missed on your own, you recite as though it is your first raka, but, you act like it is your second raka'a in terms of movements. If this was Maghrib, that means instead of standing and reciting two raka'a before sitting for the tashahhud as you would normally, you instead recite the Fatiha, a sura and the tashahhud in both raka's you are making up since in form, you sit and recite the tashahhud in the second and third raka' of every Maghrib prayer. And your recitation should be aloud in both raka'as (though not loud enough to disturb others) since it would have been aloud if you had not missed those raka'as with the imam. Likewise, if you caught only the last raka'a of Isha with the imam, you would: stand, recite the Fatiha and a sura, bow, stand, do the two sujuds and sit and perform the tashahhud. You then would stand, recite aloud the Fatiha and sura, bow, stand, do the two prostrations and then stand and complete your third individual/fourth actual raka'a as normal. In both situations, a tashahhud has to be done between your two first individual raka'as since your initial make-up raka'a would be your second actual in form. You would not sit and perform a tashahhud after your second make-up raka'a in Isha since it is actually your third raka'a in form, but you would in Maghrib because it is your last raka'a.

"An obligatory prayer is not repeated after its performance."

- This may seem to contradict what was said previously when our author said "If one prays the obligatory prayer by himself… he should pray with the congregation, intending four raka'as of voluntary prayer." A legally valid obligatory prayer is not repeated in the Hanafi School. Once the obligation has been discharged, it has been discharged and cannot be discharged again. Doing so is prohibited (makruh tahriman) as our commentator explains as a result of the Prophet's forbidding it in a hadith that is not well-known to the public, but is considered authentic by the hadith scholars. Since it is prohibited (makruh tahriman) to leave the mosque after the adhan has been called until the congregation has been performed and it is also not appropriate to repeat a prayer whose obligation has been discharged, you join the congregation with the intention of nafila since it is permissible for the follower to pray a prayer of lesser merit than the imam.

"If one joins the congregation while the imam is in the bowing position…"

- Meaning that both the takbirat al-ihram and bowing with the imam are a condition of catching that raka'a. If the imam raises his head before you are in the bowing position, that raka'a does not count and needs to be made up after the imam has completed his prayer according to the method that has already been explained.

THE PROSTRATION OF FORGETFULNESS

"If, however, he performs the prostration of the extra raka'a, his obligatory prayer is invalidated…"
- that is, if someone rises for a fifth raka'a, they should stop that raka and return to the Salat al-Ibrahimiyya and conclude their prayer unless they have reached the point of prostration in that extra raka'a. If they have, they should add another raka'a in order to keep the prayer even, but intend for these additional raka's to be nafl and the concluding salam to cover both the two nafl and original fard that they mistakenly added to.
- In addition to what our commentator mentions, a prostration for forgetfulness is also due for adding an extra integral to the prayer, since doing so entails that when one corrects their mistake, they have delayed the performance of an integral beyond what is allowed.

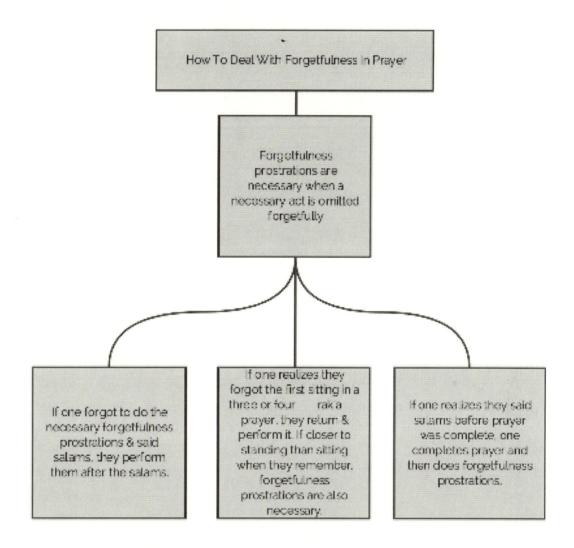

THE PROSTRATION OF RECITAL

- <u>Recall</u>: The prostration of recital takes the same ruling as the prayer with respect to the times that it can be performed. If it is heard in a time where it is makruh or unlawful to pray, it is also makruh or unlawful to perform. In such cases, it would be delayed in the karaha or prohibition of prayer is no longer in effect.

"However, hearing the verse is a condition…"

- Meaning that simply hearing the verse mandates the prostration in the Hanafi School. If you were in another part of the masjid or building and were not a part of the majlis in which the verse was recited, the mere fact that you heard it obligates your prostration, unlike in other Schools where you would not be required to prostrate if you just happened to hear the verse, but were not a part of the gathering. This is why our author says later "It is recommended to recite it silently if someone else is present and not paying attention" as not to obligate the prostration on someone who is not aware it is about to be recited or is not prepared to prostrate due to their not being part of your gathering.

"Joining the congregation in a raka'a …. Otherwise, he must perform his own prostration if he heard it from the imam."
- Meaning that if he heard it from the imam <u>before he joined the prayer,</u> as mentioned by our commentator. In that case, he should perform the prostration after the prayer since the part of the prayer where it was done was missed by him. Technically, the imam's prostration that he missed would ordinarily free him from having to perform the prostration himself, but if he heard it outside of the prayer, the obligation of him prostrating is a result of his hearing the verse being recited and has nothing to do with the prayer itself and so it is not connected to it.

"One prostration suffices for the recital … multiple times…"
- *I.e.*, if you are memorizing a sura or series of verses, you are only required to prostrate the first time that you recited the verse.

THE PROSTRATION OF GRATITUDE

"There is a difference of opinion…"
- Because the scholars disagree on whether or not the prostration of the Prophet (Allah bless him and give him peace) and his Companions out of gratitude was a spontaneous response on their part or an actual sunna that was intended to be followed. The stronger opinion is that it is a sunna, but you should not do it immediately after the prayer so that people don't confuse it with a sujud al-sahwi or think that it is specifically recommended to do sujud after the group prayer.

THE FRIDAY PRAYER

"The Friday prayer is an individual obligation…"
- "Being a freeman…" means that the individual is not a slave who is owned by another person. The original word here is "الحرية" or "freedom" and according to the meaning intended here, the opposite of "freedom" is not "incarceration," but "slavery". This is clear from other texts which mention that it is not obligatory for a "slave" and mention nothing about prisoners even though prison was an institution originally introduced by Umar ibn al-Khattab in order to force people who were able to pay their debts to pay them. Students should not make analogies of this sort on their own, especially when they relate to something as serious as the obligation of an act of worship. In order to be absolutely sure that this is the

case in the Hanafi School, we consulted a qualified mufti in Texas and this was his response (summarized):

> Prisoners are not analogous to slaves. The difference between the two is that the situation of a slave is an absolute restriction, while the restrictions placed upon prisoners is temporary as a result of the latter's commission of a crime. This can be reasoned from the fact incarceration is not a quality which is transferred to another and so the children of incarcerated individuals are not automatically considered to be prisoners themselves. As a result of these differences [many of which have been excluded for brevity], an analogy is not made between the two "types" of people. So if incarcerated Muslims have access or permission to pray Jumu`a by the prison administration, then Jumu`a is obligatory upon them. If no permission is granted by the prison administration,[12] then Jum`ah is no longer obligatory. However, if it is held unofficially, it would be valid. (Sh. Faizanul Mustafa Qadri)

- "The head of state…." is based on the concern of fitna potentially resulting when there is no one to organize the Jumu`a prayer in a city which could lead to different people (or groups) fighting over who should lead the prayer. Other Schools handled this by mandating that Jumu`a only be held in the main Jami☐ masjid of every city and it only be extended to a second masajid when the crowd becomes an issue, then a third when the second can no longer accommodate, then a fourth when the third gets full and so on. That being so, this is a condition that is not essential to Jumu`a itself. Thus, the commentator's words is what should apply in your situation (and ours in general in the US given that there is no legitimate Muslim authority). This was the position that fatwa was given upon (mufta bi-hi) in places like Southern India which were not ruled by Muslims. The Hanafi scholars still held and mandated Jumu`ah there, even though this condition was not possible to fulfill.
- "The presence of even one person…" does not seem to be the strongest opinion and so Ibn Abidin's preference should be relied upon due to his weight as the principal verifier (sahib al-tarjih) in the late-Hanafi School. If one is in a situation where there is only you and the imam, you would be permitted to follow this position out of necessity since you have no choice in where you attend the Jumu`ah prayer.
- "General permission…" is a condition that applies specifically to the prayer. Unfortunately, there is a mistaken fatwa that has been circulated in the prison system that cites this condition as a reason for the invalidity of Jumu`ah in prisons. However, upon further research, it is clear that this condition should not be applied blindly. In *Durr al-Mukhtar*,[13] Ala al-Din al-Haskafi states "Closing the door to a fort in fear of an enemy or due to an old habit will not contradict this condition, as an open permission is still in place for its inhabitants…. And it is written in *Al-Shamiyyah*[14] [that] 'Only [intentionally] preventing

---

[12] This is a general statement that is the default ruling. In our situation, due to the Constitution of the United States, the right to practice your religion cannot be prevented unless it contradicts other established laws or is unintentionally restricted due to other considerations which take precedence (like lockdown or being housed in a supermax which only allows very limited interactions for the purposes of safety).

[13] *Durr al-Mukhtar* is the core text around which *Radd al-Muhtar* was written. The combination of those two text, *Radd al-Mukhtar ala Durr al-Muhtar* has since become the central reference point for fatwa in the contemporary Hanafi School.

[14] I.e., *Radd al-Mukhtar*, since Ibn Abidin was from Damascus, his hashiya became referred to independently as *al-Shamiyya* due his near celebrity status in the School. Someone who rejects this opinion or refuses to apply it in this situation is merely being stubborn, since this very work is cited in that very same fatwa that has been circulated

worshippers [from attending the actual prayer] will contradict this condition and keeping enemies away will not." From this, we understand that "general permission" means that people are not prevented from attending the Friday prayer without reason. In the case of a prison, the fact that access to the prison has been restricted for security purposes has the side effect of preventing people outside of the prison from attending Jumu`ah is not considered since the security protocols are an unintended side-effect which does not invalidate the validity of the prayer. Jumu`a would only be invalid in the Hanafi School based upon general permission if the reason why the "gates" of the prison are locked is for the expressed purpose of keeping Muslims outside from joining Jumu`a with their incarcerated Brothers. Since this is not the case and Muslims who are incarcerated within the prison walls are generally allowed to attend Jumu`ah, this condition has not been violated. The fatwa that declared the contrary is a mistake and should be ignored. A short copy of the fatwa has been added at the end of this FIQH 112 Companion for those who would like to see it in full.

- "A congregation of [at least] three men…" seems to be a contradiction of the previously mention ruling of one person who listens to the sermon, but the subject here is the prayer after the sermon, not the sermon itself. Thus, according to the author, if at least one person is present from the beginning to end of the sermon and then two people join in time to catch the beginning of the prayer, Jumu`a is valid. But perhaps since three people are needed for the prayer, scholars like Ibn Abidin preferred that three people are present for the sermon as well.

"Any vicinity that has its own governor…"
- As mentioned above and in the commentary regarding the "head of state" appointing someone, this does not apply in your situation since the point of this ruling is to prevent fitna and infighting in the community.
-

"The minimum obligation for a valid sermon is one tasbiha…"
- The fatwa position is that the khutba must be in Arabic in the Hanafi School. Mufti Taqi Usmani gives the proof for this in his *The Language of the Friday Khutba*. However, as is evident here, merely reciting Dhikr is sufficient and so if someone were to make Dhikr, followed by salawat upon the Prophet (Allah bless him and give him peace), recite a few verses from the Qur'an and conclude with a short du`a, all in Arabic, this would be sufficient to fulfill the conditions of a valid khutba in the Hanafi School without dislike. This is what Uthman ibn Affan restricted himself to as his first Jumu`a khutba after he became the caliph and so there is no question that it is valid. Therefore, in order to maintain optimal validity and remove the difference of opinion about the matter of the language, if you are giving the khutba, you should do this in each of your two sermons. After you have done the above, there would be no problem in you giving another sermon in English. In fact, restricting yourself to Dhikr and du`a in the second sermon is the practice of many scholars of the Hanafi School who typically begin with their usual praise, recite Qur'an 33:56 and conclude the second sermon with a du`a in Arabic.

"Once the imam emerges…"

---

which declares Jumu`ah to be invalid. This is why and how we can state so bluntly that the opinion which declares it invalid in the Hanafi School to be a mistake.

FIQH 112: RITUAL PRAYER (SALAT)

- Refraining from everything but listening to the khutba is obligatory once the imam steps on the mimbar and gives the salams. This includes tahiyyat al-masjid, which is prohibited and invalid while the imam is on the mimbar. If someone is not aware of the difference of opinion over this and insists that you stand and pray, simply ignore them politely and explain to them that there is a difference among the scholars on this point if they try to make an issue out of it later.

"If one joins the Friday prayer in the tashahhud…"
- This is even though you have not technically caught the raka'a if you did not join when the imam was bowing based on the fact that you have technically "caught" the prayer with your takbirat al-ihram if you perform it while the imam is still praying or prior to the time of any prayer ending. However, in terms of make-up, it simply doesn't count. So though you did not catch the raka'a, you caught the Jumu'a prayer and so you pray it as a Jumu'ah prayer when you rise to make up what you missed.

THE 'ID PRAYER

- If a Hanafi is performing the Id prayer behind an imam who follows a different school of fiqh, you simply follow him in the manner that he peforms the prayer since the number of takbirs mentioned in the text is only one of preference, not validity, as long as they do not exceed more than 17 takbirs (which none of the Four Canonical Schools do).

"It is recommended to add…"
- The Arabic of this is found in the appendix on page 196.

THE PRAYER OF FEAR

- The prayer is only performed in this manner by members of the community who are engaged in warfare in the heat of battle when there is not enough of a pause in fighting to safely perform the obligatory prayer. This should not be an issue in the prison setting. The place where the prayer is performed in a community should be secure enough that this situation is not warranted. If there is an active threat to the entire community, then the prison administration should be compelled by law to ensure that the place where religious activities are held is safe.

THE FUNERAL PRAYER AND BURIAL

"This is referred to as talqin and it is also performed after his burial."
- This is not a practical issue inside prison, but some people make it a point over which others are declared "Ahl al-Bid'a." Though some scholars may consider this to be a bid'a, there is proof for it and no single individual's opinion invalidates the opinions of other mujtahid scholars. As the commentator says, those who wish to participate in it may participate in it and those who do not believe that it is legislated should refrain without either side condemning or considering the other to be sinful. This is the case with all

matters that are disagreed upon by the scholars for which there is no decisive proof.[15] Since this is not particularly relevant inside prisons, the rest of the commentary will be skipped, though you should still read and study this section.

MARTYRS

- As the commentator mentions, this is discussing martyrs in the legal sense. As for the hadith, "Martyrdom is even things beside being killed for the sake of Allah. The one who dies of a plague is a martyr, the one who drowns is a martyr, the one who dies of lung complications is a martyr, the one who dies of a stomach disease is a martyr, the one who dies in a fire is a martyr, the one who does in a collapsed building is a martyr and the woman who dies in pregnancy is a martyr." (Abu Dawud) This hadith is accepted, but is not acted upon - *i.e.*, these people will be raised as martyrs in the Afterlife (in sha Allah), but they are not buried as martyrs in this world. The honor of this burial is only reserved for those who died in battle or was killed defending themselves or their family from an active threat.

---

[15] NOTE: The mere fact that there is a disagreement among qualified scholars should be evidence enough to those who are not trained in religious disciplines that there is no decisive proof for either opinion.

Fasting (Sawm)

"Fasting is to withhold from eating, drinking and sexual intercourse during daylight hours…"

- This means that it is permissible to eat, drink and have intercourse with one's spouse from sunset until true dawn, as the commentator mentions. There is a common misconception that many people have due to their misinterpreting the hadith that is mentioned by the commentator. Some people have mistaken the hadith to mean that you may eat until the adhan is called for Fajr, even if the adhan is called accidentally or intentionally late. Fasting becomes incumbent when true dawn enters, not at sunrise. This idea has managed to get into people's mind that essentially considers beginning the fast at daybreak to be Sunna, while eating after sunrise is haram. So many think that they are permitted to eat after Subh has entered if they accidently overslept suhur, for example, as long as the sun has not yet risen. That is not the case. The "night" in Arabic begins at Maghrib and the "day" at Subh. "Daylight" means that the light of the sun is visible in the sky and does not refer to the period between sunrise and sunset as it is customarily used in English. Rulings are based on what is understood from the Arabic at the time of the Revelation, not what they may imply in other languages. This is why learning Arabic is essential for understanding our religion.

- There is also an unnecessary controversy raised over the issue of imsak due to a similar misunderstanding a related hadith. Imam Bukhari narrates that Zayd ibn Thabit said "We made suhur with the Prophet (Allah bless him and give him peace) and then he stood for prayer." Anas ibn Malik asked Zayd, "What was the time between suhur and the adhan?" Zayd ibn Thabit replied, "The time was sufficient to recite fifty verses from the Qur'an." This hadith can be interpreted two different ways and each of them are valid. If you interpret the question as "What is the amount of time between when you began suhur and the adhan was called?" Then it would mean that it took the Prophet the amount of time it would take to recite 50 verses to eat suhur. This would mean that the Prophet (Allah bless him and give him peace) ate right up until the time of Subh. However, if you interpret the question to mean "What was the amount of time between when suhur was completed and the adhan for Subh was called?" it would mean that there was a brief period of time between when the Prophet (Allah bless him and give him peace) stopped eating and when Subh began. This latter interpretation is the interpretation of Abu Hanifa (and Malik). Thus it is recommended in the Hanafi School to stop eating around 10 minutes prior to Subh beginning. The fact that it is permissible to eat until Subh does not mean doing so is obligatory. Those who claim that doing imsak is "extremism" or "an innovation" are in error. The Salaf did not accuse each other of innovation for having differences of opinion. That being said, it is also an error for people to declare that it is haram to eat after the "time of imsak" or to force others to stop as though they are doing something objectionable when Subh has not yet entered. Imsak is only recommended and eating right up until Subh is permissible as long as there is no doubt whether or not Subh has begun.[1] Turning a recommendation into an obligation is also a bid`a and is perhaps a worse option than considering established differences of opinion to be innovations. It remains recommended to stop eating 10 minutes before Subh and if someone blames you

---

[1] *I.e.*, you should not eat right up to the minute that is posted in the prayer calendar since that time is not necessarily correct, as we discussed in the previous chapter. This is also why the commentator recommends the 18 degree calculation for fasting, instead of the 15 degree calculation since 18 degrees results in an earlier time and is more precautionary for individuals who are not able to observe the entrance of Subh themselves.

or accuses you of innovation for performing imsak, make du'a for them, politely ignore their mistakes and **"Do not fear the blame of a critic."** (Qur'an 5:54)
- "Obligatory… fasts of expiation and vowed fasts … according to the more apparent position" is actually an opinion that was overturned by later scholars, as the commentator states. The fact that kaffara and nadhr fasts are wajib and not fard is only a technical difference. According to either opinion, the individual is obliged to perform them and if they do not, they are liable to be punished in the Afterlife. <u>RECALL</u>: The difference between something being fard and wajib in the Hanafi School is tied to its rejection being kufr or merely sinful. In terms of practice and personal implementation, there is virtually no difference between the two categories.
- "Mandatory: makes up of broken voluntary fasts…" means that once you begin a voluntary fast in the Hanafi School, you are obliged to complete it since the Qur'an says **"Make not vain your deeds"** (Qur'an 47:33) and this is taken to be a general rule that once an act of worship is begin, it must be completed unless extenuating circumstances occur. However, doing so for a valid reason is acceptable, but requires make-up. The details of this are mentioned in later sections.
- "Sunna: the fasting of the Blessed Ashura" is unfortunately a Sunna that has perhaps been lost in many communities. Due to the martyrdom of Husayn (Allah be well pleased with him) being reported on this day, many Muslims have turned it from a day of celebration to a day of mourning or at the very least feel sad on this day. This is the very definition of a bid'a. The Prophet (Allah bless him and give him peace) fasted the Day of Ashura and commanded the Muslims to fast it as well. (Muslim) Likewise, Amr ibn al-As said, "Whoever fasts the 10th of Muharram it is as though he has fasted the entire year. And whoever gives charity on the 10th of Muharram, it is like he has given charity the entire year." (Ibn Rajab, *Lata'if al-Ma'arif*) He would not have said this had he not heard it from the Prophet, who is reported to have said "One who generously spends on his family on the 10th of Muharram, Allah will be generous on him for the entire year." (Tabarani, Bayhaqi) It is firmly established that Ashura is a day of celebration from the Prophet's own instruction. Historically, Muslims used to fast this day, spend freely on their family and give gifts to their children with a similar community spirit as what happens during Eid. Nothing abrogates the Sunna of the Prophet but the Prophet himself. As for Husayn ibn Ali (Allah be well pleased with both of them) being martyred on this day, their sanctity is not above the sanctity of the Prophet (Allah bless him and give him peace) and he very well knew that Husayn would be martyred. And what does Allah Most High say of the martyrs? **"And say not of those who have been slain in the way of Allah: 'They are dead.' Nay! They are living, though [you] perceive it not."** (Qur'an 2:154) This was said in response to the Muslims who were intensely mourning those who had been slain at Badr. This verse was an admonition to those who were mourning the martyrs by saying "Why are you crying over those who are receiving their ultimate reward with Me? If you really understood, you would mourn over yourselves and desire to have the same fate as they." While it may be true that it was a sad day of Muslim history, with Allah and from Husayn's point of view, it was the greatest thing that Husayn could have been gifted with. So there is no reason for anyone to be sorrowful on the Day of Ashura, other than those who had the misfortune to be raised on the Day of Judgment as having been responsible for killing the Prophet's (Allah bless him and give him peace) beloved grandson. And there is most certainly no legal grounds for this day to be considered a "Day of Mourning" and the Sunna of the Prophet and his Companions be neglected.
- "478. Although some scholars considered it recommended to fast on Friday…" since it was established that Ibn Abbas used to fast on Friday alone, even though he was aware of the hadith forbidding it. From

this, we can understand that the Prophet's (Allah bless him and give him peace) command to fast the Thursday before or Saturday after Friday was a temporary prohibition which only applied in Madina. This was because when the Muslims were living side-by-side with Jews, the latter considered themselves to be religious authorities and in order to make it clear to them that the Prophet (Allah bless him and give him peace) superseded them, he began recommending certain things to the Muslims in order to make a distinction between the two communities. Once the religion of Islam was established and the separation between the Muslims and Jews was made, that concern was no longer an issue. So according to what appears to be the stronger opinion, once the underlying reason for the prohibition was no longer a concern, the prohibition itself was lifted. That being said, both opinions are valid. But Friday being a meritorious day for the Muslims is clearly established and so many of the Hanafi and Maliki scholars considered it recommended to fast it on its own in order to honor the day.

- "Mildly Disliked… Nayruz or Mahrajan…" because many of the Hanafis were Persian and they had been used to honoring Nayruz and Mahrajan in their previous religious culture. The same, therefore, would likely apply to us who used to be Christian. Fasting intentionally on Christmas or Eastern is something we should avoid since these are not days that we should honor.

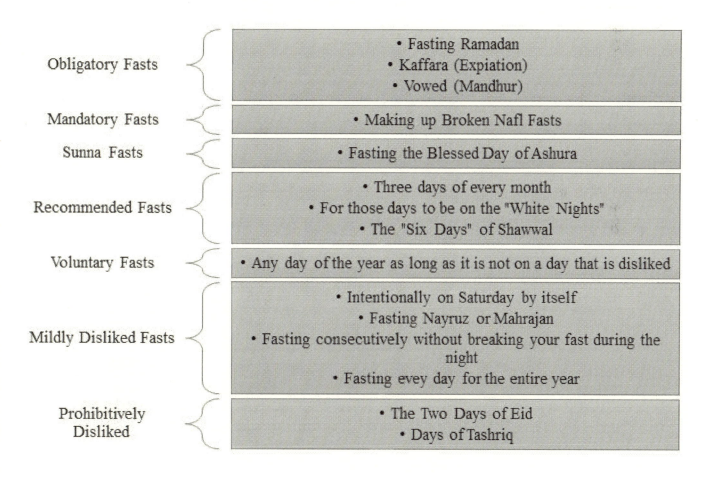

FIQH 112: FASTING (SAWM)

THE INTENTION OF FASTING

[All types of fasts require an intention…. As well as that the intention be made the previous night before fajr, yet after maghrib.]
- *I.e.*, it is not permissible in the Hanafi School to begin any obligatory or wajib fast in the middle of the day, excluding the regular fast of Ramadan.

"The following types of fasts… the intention may be made any time from the previous night until dahwa kubra"
- In case it was not clear in the commentary, dahwa kubra is the midpoint of the sun's visibility in the sky. So if sunrise (shuruq) beings at 6 am and sunset (Maghrib) begins at 8 pm, it would be permissible to retroactively begin the fast of Ramadan, specified vows and nafl fasts before 1 pm as long as you have not done anything that would render the fast invalid. In the case of Ramadan, fasting it is obligatory, but someone may not have been aware that Ramadan had actually begun.

THE CRESCENT MOON

"The beginning of the month of Ramadan is established by…"
- Meaning that relying on calculations for the beginning and ending of Ramadan is not permissible in the Hanafi School. Therefore, if one's community has decided to establish Ramadan based on calculations which do not coincide with physical sighting or the completion of the previous month, following them is not valid. Also, both regional and global sighting is valid in the Hanafi School as long as the global sighting occurs during the night and it is verified to be reliable. For the reason that the latter is difficult to do as a global institution, the fatwa that most contemporary Hanafis follow is actually regional sighting even though the stronger opinion is the binding obligation of global observation.[2] This does not mean that you make an argument out of it, but you quietly follow your own school whenever sighting and calculation does not coincide. If you are put in the situation where the community has begun their fast a day before you have, because the moon was not actually sighted, then leave them to their opinion and do not make an issue out of it. If the same happens during Eid, then you should celebrate with them, while maintaining your fast until the moon of Shawwal has been sighted. There have been many times I have celebrated Eid with the community while fasting and then prayed Eid by myself the next day in the privacy of my own home since the community I used to live in decided to follow calculations as their established method. I do not think anyone realized that I was still fasting except one individual who

---

[2] This is because it is difficult to verify sightings that have occurred in all corners of the globe. This fact was made evident in 2017 when sightings were claimed in parts of Africa that many people insisted should be followed and based their declaration of Ramadan upon and after a bit of research was done, it was determined that all of these reports were unreliable and should have been rejected. Al-hamdu li-Llah, in this situation, the valid sightings did eventually occur in South America, so it was not an issue. But it demonstrates the wisdom of the Hanafi scholars who refused to switch to a global system since they did not have reliable contacts in every corner of the globe.

suspected it, but I refused to confirm his suspicions. I imagine that the same has probably happened on occasion to everyone else on the Tayba staff.

"One may not fast on the Day of Doubt…"
- *I.e.*, unless you are genuinely fasting it as a voluntary fast and not "just in case it is Ramadan".

"If there is no obstruction… there must be a large body of people that sight the new crescent."
- This is tawatur that has been mentioned in ISLAM 99 and IMAN 101.[3] It produces certainty and so in the hadith science, it is beyond requiring authentication, in aqida establishes fundamental beliefs and in fiqh is considered undeniable proof of something having occurred.

"Moonsighting for `Id al-Adhan, as well as every lunar month…"
- Which is to say that the moon should be visibly sighted and confirmed for each and every month, not just Ramadan. The only difference between Sha'ban and Ramadan is that since they are each needed in order to establish the accuracy of Ramadan's arrival, the criterion is a tad bit stricter.

THINGS THAT INVALIDATE THE FAST

If one eats or drinks something of nutritional value or something for medicinal purposes…"
- Anything that has nutritional benefit that is <u>consumed</u> breaks the fast. The same applies to asthma inhalers or vaporized steroid treatments. They are nutritional in that they benefit the body and enter it through the main cavity. If one has asthma and a doctor permits you to change the timing of their dosages around the fast time, then you are obliged to fast despite your condition. The same applies if you only need on it an emergency basis. However, if your asthma is so severe that going without your normal treatment would put you in a state of distress, fasting would not be permissible for you and has to be made up if and when it would be safe to do so.[4] Likewise if you start to have breathing problems and need it to breath normally again. It breaks your fast, but breaking it under these circumstances would be obligatory and only a qada would be owed. Any chronic condition that renders one unable to fast due to it negatively affecting their

---

[3] As of Fall 2017, IMAN 101 was introduced as a new course and ISLAM 99 is scheduled for either Spring or Fall of 2018. So those of you who are taking the first version of this course may not know what I am referring to. To be brief, tawatur is a form of transmission which implies that a large group of people were witnesses to something so large that it is impossible for them to have conspired to lie or all have made the same mistake. Therefore, according to usul al-fiqh, a mutawatir narration is undeniable and anyone who rejects it is guilty of kufr. This is because tawatur is how the Qur'an reached us and therefore someone who denies tawatur is the same as someone who rejected the Prophet (Allah bless him and give him peace) to his face. So for fiqh, tawatur of the sighting of the crescent is undeniable and obligates everyone to follow it. The mere fact that a large group of people may be fasting does not establish tawatur unless this group of people actually saw the moon themselves. "I heard that the moon was sighted in such-and-such land" is not what is meant by tawatur, but "So-and-so, so-and-so, so-and-so, so-and-so, so-and-so, so-and-so, so-and-so, *etc.*, <u>all declared</u> that they had sighted the moon" is what is meant by tawatur. Also, if the Muslim authorities of the land have declared Ramadan to have begun and ended, then everyone <u>in that land</u> is obliged to follow them. If they are incorrect, the mistake is on the heads of the government and not the people. Anyone who does not begin and end their fast according to the government's declaration is disobedient. This only applies to the people who live in those places. It is not valid for someone living in the United States to begin or end their fast based upon what is done in Saudi Arabia (for example) unless it is a result of their having cited the moon-.

[4] Likewise with people who are on antibiotics because they are trying to get over a bacterial infection.

health makes you akin to the elderly and so you are excused from fasting unless you happen to recover from that condition. This is very common with diabetics. If someone has diabetes so severe that not eating would put them into insulin shock or eventually cause harm to their body, fasting is actually prohibited and you are liable to be punished for harming yourself if you try to fast anyway. Unfortunately, many elderly people (and diabetics) who are used to fasting attempt to fast even when doing so is dangerous because they feel that they are "missing out" on Ramadan.[5] However, a woman who is on her menstrual period, her fasting (and prayer) is haram, which necessarily means that she is being rewarded when she refrains from doing so. The person who is not permitted to fast and complies is in the same perpetual state of obedience during the day as the person who is obliged to fast and does. No one should feel that they are "less spiritual" or "missing out" when they are unable to fast because of their health. No state of obedience should be considered "less spiritual" than another because it outwardly seems inferior. It is similar to the Prophet's (Allah bless him and give him peace) clarification that no one should think that the nabuwwa of Yunus was inferior to his own nabuwwa because his was received in Mount Hira and Prophet Yunus' was received in the belly of a fish. An act of obedience is an act of obedience and the relationship that each individual has with their Lord is uniquely their own. In the event that you suffer from a chronic condition that makes fasting impermissible for you, you should follow what is mentioned about the elderly on page 135.

- "If one has sexual intercourse in either of the two passages on purpose…" *i.e.*, if someone is unfortunately the victim of rape while they are fasting, their fast is broken due to the fact that they "had" intercourse, but since they did so unwillingly, it only requires a makeup and they are not considered sinful for having been raped or having been forced to break their fast.

"Those that require a makeup without expiation…"

- "Something not normally eaten like dirt, reaching the body cavity…" since anything which reaches the body cavity intentionally breaks the fast. But in this case, when it is not nutritional, it does not mandate a kaffara. However, this does not pertain to smoking cigarettes (or worse substances). Because cigarettes can be refrained from and they include nicotine which has a stimulating effect on the brain, anyone who intentionally smokes during the day of Ramadan owes both a makeup and an expiation. Someone who states the contrary has violated the consensus of the scholars. Due to the presence of the substances in the smoke which have chemical effects on the brain and bloodstream, cigarette smoke is not treated like incense since incense has no actual effect on the body and it is not akin to asthma inhalers since the latter are permissible and frequently needed in order to prevent breathing difficulties which would pose a hardship. So if someone is addicted to cigarettes, they should try to wean themselves off before Ramadan so they do not have to simultaneously deal with hunger and nicotine withdrawal symptoms. And in the case of asthma inhalers, there are some people who have declared that they do not break the fast, but this opinion goes against the principles of the Hanafi School. So while it may not be as objectionable as fatwas declaring smoking to be permitted during Ramadan, it should still be ignored.

---

[5] For example, the wife of one of the imams that I know almost permanently blinded herself one Ramadan due to her fasting against her doctor's orders and that of her husband (who was a scholar). Towards the end of Ramadan, her diabetes flared up so badly that she lost her vision. Al-hamdu li-Llah, it returned once she was hospitalized and given treatment, but she never should have begun fasting to begin with and it was not a guarantee that her situation was possible to reverse. This was following the previous Ramadan where she also fell sick and almost went into insulin shock for the very same reason.

- "Accidentally swallowing water while rinsing the mouth" because this should have been avoidable, it is not treated like forgetfully eating. The same applies to someone who accidently swallowed water while taking a shower. It is not considered like forgetfully drinking since it is something that you should have not done during the day in a way which could have potentially violated your fast. The same goes for swimming (unless you are a lifeguard who is attempting to save someone's life).[6]
- "Eating in the daytime…" applies to the situations mentioned previously in which forming an intention is not required for certain types of fasts as long as they are intended before midday. If began their fast, but recalled that they had eaten early in the morning, their fast is broken and it is not treated like someone who forgetfully ate while fasting.
- "Someone pouring water into the body cavity of a sleeping person…" may seem to be an odd condition to mention, but recall that Abu Hanifa and his circle was famous for issuing rulings on theoretical situations. Though some scholars condemned this, their having done so meant that later scholars had an entire body of precedents upon which to pass fatwas for newly occurring situations. This is one of those rulings and it is mentioned in the works of the Hanafis because it demonstrates a principle that anything which breaks the fast, but which was not done intentionally or is something that is outside of the norm, requires a makeup, but no expiation (kaffara).

- **"502 Intentionally inhaling smoke… If, however, one unintentionally inhales or ingests smoke…"** Means that if one has a cellmate or is in an area where someone else is smoking, you unintentionally inhaling their smoke does not break your fast since smoke is something that is not possible to avoid once it is in the air. And when the commentator says "If one inhales smoke with enjoyment or for benefit, then both a makeup and expiation are required" this is proof of what we said above about cigarettes breaking the fast and requiring a kaffara.

Those that require nothing and are not disliked…"
- "Blood cupping or drawing blood" refers to a practice that is part of Eastern and Prophetic medicine in which blood that is considered "stale" is drawn towards the skin and removed from the body. It is not "bloodletting" which Europeans used to do because they used to believe that illness was the result of demons possessing people. Someone may think that if ingesting breaks the fast, so should removing, but that is not the case. Doing so is not even disliked unless you feel it would weaken you. So although "drawing blood" is mentioned here, this does not refer to donating blood, which is a contemporary practice. The amount of blood which is extracted when it is donated is enough to cause fatigue, which is why you are given fluids and allowed to rest in the bed immediately after you donate blood in order for the nurses to make sure that you are safe to leave and will not fall unconscious in the middle of the street after you leave their presence. So unless you know from experience that you are those rare individuals who are not affected by drawing blood, it should be avoided during the day of Ramadan.
- "Using a toothstick" in the opinion of some scholars should be avoided after a certain time since they argue that it freshens the breath and the Prophet (Allah bless him and give him peace) said "By the One in Whose Hand is my soul, the breath of the fasting person is more pleasant with Allah than the smell of musk." (Bukhari) However, the smell of the breath of a fasting person does not come from their mouth,

---

[6] In which case you still would need to make up the fast, but the fact that you were trying to save someone's life should be sufficient enough reason to remove the sinfulness of what would otherwise be considered negligent.

but from the fact that their stomach has been empty for so long, yet is full of stomach acids that are waiting to break down food. As a result, the Hanafis argue that the general recommendation of using the miswak remains even during Ramadan, since using a dry miswak has very little effect on one's breath.

"Those that require nothing yet are disliked…"

- If one tastes some food… 505. unless there is a valid excuse, such as a woman tasting the food she cooks because her husband is unkind…" is an example of the Sacred Law taking the reality of people's situation into consideration. There are unfortunately many men who are extremely selfish and demanding of their wives and if a woman is married to such an individual, the likely consequences of her husband's anger is excuse enough for the karaha of this situation to be removed. This does not mean that a woman has to obey her husband in everything, even if it is unreasonable. Rather, it means that if a woman has to do something in order to keep her husband from harming her or making her life difficult, then she does so out of necessity. For situations that are worse than this, a woman should consult her local scholar to see what her options are in her particular situation.

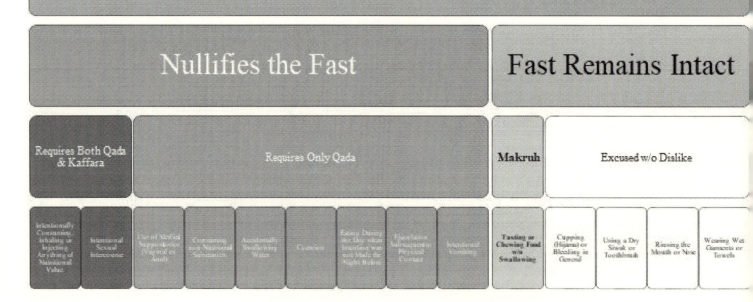

"The following actions of the day necessitate withholding (imsak)…"

- "If one breaks the fast…" means that if you break your fast, unless you did so for health reasons, you are not permitted to eat. The sanctity (hurma) of Ramadan necessitates that eating, drinking and sexual intercourse be refrained from by those upon whom it is obligatory to do so. The fact that you may have violated this sanctity does not mean that the obligation of refraining from eating, drinking and sexual intercourse has been removed.
- "If a woman in menstruation becomes pure…" for the same reason as a traveller who becomes a resident: the sanctity of the month and the fact that they would have been obligated to fast had they been in this

condition when the day began. However, when the opposite situation occurs (*i.e.*, a woman who was fasting begins to menstruate), she is not required to do imsak and actually doing so can be considered haram since it is like she is still fasting when doing so is unlawful and invalid. In this latter situation, there is no reason why she should perform imsak.
- "The first three require a makeup, as opposed to the last two" because in the case of the last two (the new Convert and the new adult), they were not obliged to fast when the day began and so there is nothing for them to make up.[7]

EXEMPTIONS FROM FASTING

"The following people are exempted…"
- "Or a traveller, yet for him to fast is more preferable…" since it is established that the Prophet (Allah bless him and give him peace) fasted while he was travelling and the evidence suggests that he only broke his fast to demonstrate that doing so was permissible. But since Ramadan has a sanctity that other months do not have, making up a fast outside of Ramadan is not the same as fasting it at its proper time whenever someone has a choice to do so. As for the assertion that fasting while travelling is a difficult and so it is recommended to leave, then the reply is that fasting itself is a difficulty and there is some difficulty that we have to put up with as a consequence of the very concept of religion. A religion without any demands or expectations is not a religion, but hedonism and delusion. Also, please remember what the commentator says about the conditions of breaking the fast while travelling which we have already discussed in the previous chapter.

"A person performing a voluntary fast may break it…"
- Whenever you read "according to one narration" this is often a sign that the opinion being narrated is weak or at least not preferred. That is the case here, as the commentator clarified. The relied upon position is that once someone begins a voluntary fast, it is obligatory to complete it for the reasons that we mentioned above. However, in this case, not waking up for suhur is considered to be a valid excuse since this particular fast is not obligatory and fasting without having performed suhur may make the fast difficult outside of Ramadan when you likely have not been eating according to a schedule conducive to fasting. Another valid excuse is mentioned in the next line.

SPIRITUAL RETREAT IN THE MOSQUE

The spiritual retreat is of three types…"
- "Emphasized Communal Sunna…" because just as there are things which are fard ayn and fard kifaya, there are things which are sunna ayn and sunna kifaya. As for the sunna ayn, it is everything that has been described thus far as "sunna mu'akkada". These are individual sunnas that must be performed by

---

[7] Technically, a non-Muslim is obliged to fast, but doing so is not valid in the opinion of some scholars. But this is a technical point that we will not get into at this time. It relates more to aqida, but has implications in fiqh that are not particularly practical since the end result is the same.

everyone, lest they individually be considered sinful. But `itikaf in the Masjid, it is a sunna kifaya since there was always someone in the Prophet's Mosque who was doing `itikaf and it is a communal institution which should occur during Ramadan. But requiring `itikaf to be performed by every single individual would pose a hardship to men and women who have to work or women who are housewives and need to take care of young children.

"The minimum period of time to fulfill a voluntary retreat…in a mosque of congregation."

- *I.e.*, one can intend a nafl `itikaf once they enter the masjid to pray for as long as they plan on remaining there. 'Itikaf is only valid in a proper Masjid in the Hanafi School for men. There is a difference of opinion on whether or not it has to be a jami☐ masjid in which all five congregational prayers are held, but this is not enough of a difference for `itikaf to be valid in the Hanafi School while one is in prison since one of the conditions of a masjid is that the property has been permanent designated as a place of prayer, Qur'an recital and Dhikr. Technically speaking, the prison "masjid" is a musalla and `itikaf would therefore not be valid there for men according to the relied upon opinion of the Hanafi School.[8]

---

[8] We are still searching to see if there is a valid opinion that men can follow in this regard. By consensus of all Four Canonical Schools, `itikaf is only valid in a Masjid where congregational prayers are held for men. However, the Hanafi and Hanbali Schools allow women to do `itikaf in their home since they are not obliged to attend the congregational prayer. We are therefore seeing if an exception has been made for men who are not able to attend the Masjid on the same grounds.

Almsgiving (Zakat)

Since this chapter is not particularly relevant for the vast majority of our students, we will only comment on the most important points that may not be clear and will not be commenting as much as we have in previous chapters since very few people will meet the conditions of being obligated to pay zakat al-mal.

"Zakat is defined as the transfer of ownership…"

- As the author states in his other famous work, *Nur al-Idah*, transfer of ownership means that the individual is given full rights of possession and control over the wealth that is being transferred to them. It is not valid to give zakat to someone on the condition that it is spent in such-and-such a manner, since that entails that full control has not been handed over. In the event that zakat is given and conditions on how it is spent has been attached, the condition is batil and is ignored.
- "Nisab above is of two types…" means that there is a nisab which establishes when one is obliged to pay zakat and a nisab when one is no longer eligible to receive it. The only difference between the two is that possessions which are not considered "wealth" in terms of nisab for paying zakat are considered with respect to the nisab of receiving it. That is because zakat is supposed to be paid to the poor in order to help them get off of their feet and someone who has property which has value that places him/her above the zakatable minimum is not considered poor since if they sold their property, they would be automatically wealthy and thus in society, their property is considered a form of stored wealth, even if it is not technically subject to zakat being taken from it.
- "…over which a full lunar year has passed…" means that if one's savings dips below the zakatable minimum at any time during the year, the fact that it may be above it when one first began counting is irrelevant. If it dips below the nisab, once it raising back above it, the year resets.
- "… in excess of any debts…" applies to debts that are owed. In the event of long term debts, they are treated like bills and only what is due currently is deducted. If someone, for example, purchased a house (with a halal mortgage of course) that was worth $500,000, but one's monthly "payment" was only $800 a month, one's debts are considered based upon that and not the remaining balance of the mortgage.[1] Even though one is technically "poor" until this debt is paid off, consideration is given to the "cash on hand".

"The nisab of gold…"

---

[1] Here, we do not mean that only halal mortgages are deducted, but that we do not agree that conventional mortgages are permissible except under dire necessity (an example being someone having to chose between homelessness for their children and buying a house with a conventional bank loan).

- In the Hanafi School, zakat is taken upon gold and silver, irrespective of the form it happens to be in, since gold and silver are considered to be money intrinsically. This is relevant to women especially, since they often have gold and silver jewellry. While some may criticize the Hanafis for this position, this is also a very intuitive position since in many cultures, women store their wealth in their gold and silver jewelry. This is the case with Arab women, who in places like Dubai and Qatar still have the habit of wearing massive amounts of gold around their necks under their abayas. This is also the case with Indians and Pakistanis who are given a gift of gold by their parents or grandparents upon getting married, which serves as a security blanket for their daughter/granddaughter. It is immediately formed into jewellry so there can be no question of who it belongs to. The intention of this gift is in the event a need arises, the wife can melt down her jewellry, sell the gold bar and have immediately have a enough cash on her hand to get through the crisis. Even women in Western countries consider their jewelry to be a part of their wealth. So Abu Hanifa and his School reasoned that, at least with gold and silver, since it has intrinsic value, it is considered wealth even though it may be in the form of personal property. This is based both on the their juridical reasoning and the fact that there are numerous examples of the female Companions, who when asked to give money for charity, removed their gold necklaces and rings and placed them in the Prophet's (Allah bless him and give him peace) hand in order for him to sell and use the money to purchase whatever he needed the money for. This is also why it was so dangerous for women to travel in the Arabian Peninsula. They were subject to getting robbed, since highway robbers knew that they literally had 10s of thousand of dollar of gold hidden under their dresses.

"The zakat of livestock…"
- Since this work was intended on being a summary, the author does not provide the breakdowns like he does in *Nur al-Idah*. Therefore, we have followed up this chapter with the relevant lines from Imam Mawsili's explanation of zakat in his *Al-Mukhtar li al-Fatawa*.

ELIGIBLE RECIPIENTS OF ZAKAT

- "A indigent person (faqir) who has no wealth at all" is usually defined as someone who does not have enough food to get them through the day.
- "A person in debt" in the Hanafi School, the nature of the debt is not considered. So even if someone happened to fall into a debt which included unlawful conditions (i.e., an interest-based loan), zakat can be given to them in order to help free them from their debtor. As long as someone has wealth below the zakatable minimum, how they may have gotten there is not considered. Also, remember that we said in the beginning that zakat is a transfer of full control and ownership over the money, so you cannot actually stipulate "I will give you this zakat if you pay off your debts" but it is given to them and they are obligated to spend it to pay off as much debt as they are able to pay without putting themselves back into the situation of destitution. That being said, if the debtor authorizes you to pay the debt off on their behalf with an understanding that the zakat actually belongs to them, this is permissible and valid as the commentator states in footnote 550.
- "A wayfarer who … has nothing on his journey" does not include someone who has enough money to put them over the nisab at home <u>if they have access to it</u>. In our times, this would exclude many people from

developed countries, since they typically possess debit/check cards which give them access to their bank account from anywhere which accepts electronic transactions.

"The one paying zakat can choose to give it to..."
- Meaning that they one paying zakat can give their zakat to anyone they wish and cannot be pressured or shamed into giving it to any particular person. Everyone who is eligible is equally deserving of the funds.
- "Zakat may not be given to…"
- "A non-Muslim" is general and unconditional. The category of "people whose hearts are inclined to Islam" was abrogated by Umar due to the spread of Islam and his understanding the intentions behind such a condition. Though the author mentions these people in *Nur al-Idah*, the commentaries clarify that Umar ibn al-Khattab in fact considered this category of people to be abrogated, since he considered the fact of Islam's spread outside of the Hijaz and the consequences of that being witnessed in those societies to be sufficient proof for anyone of how the religion of Islam takes care of the poor and needy without being unfair to those who possess significant wealth.
- "A wealthy person, *i.e.*, one who possess the nisab…" means that poverty and wealth, with respect to zakat are those who don't have the nisab and those who do - excluding the state tax collectors who are compensated for their lost review as a result of collecting zakat from people.
- "One's parents or grandparents…" since you are obliged to provide for them if they are without means and therefore, giving zakat to them is like giving zakat to yourself. The same applies to children, grandchildren, husbands and wives, which are the next to categories.
- "One's slave… one's partially-freed slave" for the exact same reason. Setting an amount for freedom with one's slave, giving your zakat to him and which would mean that he turns around and gives it back to you is nothing more than playing a game with Allah's religion.
- "Or to purchase a slave to be freed…" if you want to buy a slave in order to free them, you should buy them with your personal wealth and free them or help them make a contract with their owners and then give them your zakat so that they can free themselves.[2]

"If one makes an honest effort to pay zakat… and then finds out that the recipient was not eligible…"
- Since unlike general charity, zakat must only be paid to those who are in need. In the event that someone tried to ensure that the individual being given zakat was eligible, but then finds out that they have been deceived, the one who made an earnest attempt is not held accountable for having been deceived. This excludes the slave, since the zakat he unknowingly paid to the slave will either be returned to him as part of his manumission payment or free him from having to spend that amount of money on his slave's upkeep and so paying it out to another individual would not entail hardship.

"It is disliked to give an amount of wealth … such that he would own the nisab…"

---

[2] As for this being implemented in our times, since slavery is officially illegal in every land, no one should purchase slaves with the intention of freeing them since you will likely be accused of engaging in slavery. Additionally, once criminals find out that there is someone willing to buy slaves, they will be motivated to kidnap people in order for them to be sold - as happened in Southern Sudan when Christian missionaries began buying slaves from rural tribes in order to free them, but inadvertently created a market for slavery which funded the arming of these tribes illegal militias.

- Since this would entail that you have given so much that you have made the individual wealthy. Instead, you should give them enough zakat to them for their needs to be fulfilled and if you have remaining zakat that needs to be paid, to give it to someone else so that more than one person can be lifted from dire poverty.

"It is more preferable to give zakat to one's relatives…"
- In part because you are more likely to know their need and it will free them from having to beg or have their financial situation exposed to others outside of the family. People are more inclined to accept money from their family members than others. The same would apply to neighbors, since you generally know the financial situation of your neighbor and they have rights over you similar to that of family.

CHARITY AT THE END OF RAMADAN

"Zakat al-fitr is mandatory on every free Muslim… possessing the nisab"
- This is the Hanafi opinion which is a much greater threshold than the other Schools. In essence, it identifies everyone who is at least not eligible to receive zakat, whether they are obliged to pay it or not, which is how the Hanafis define poverty (as mentioned above).

"It is mandatory on behalf of…"
- *I.e.*, anyone who is entirely dependent upon you for their daily survival. If one has children who have their own wealth or who are working, you are not responsible for paying on their behalf.

"It is not mandatory on behalf of…"
- *I.e.*, anyone who is not dependent upon you for their daily survival. But the fact that it is not mandatory does not mean you are not permitted to pay it on their behalf, whether that be a husband for his wife or a wife for her husband.

"It is permissible to pay the monetary value…"
- This is known as the "qima" and is the famous Hanafi opinion that many people give fatwa upon, though most seem to do so because they consider money to be more beneficial than food.[3] In situations where it is not difficult for people to find food, paying the monetary value is considered superior on the grounds that it is more beneficial. However, those paying zakat al-fitr while incarcerated are likely in the latter category, since it is usually easier and causes less problems on both the one paying and one receiving of grain. That being said, since the standard of who must pay zakat al-fitr is so high in the Hanafi School, it is unlikely that many people will be obliged to pay it to begin with.

---

[3] That being said, having been the recipient of zakat al-fitr in the past, I can testify to the fact that due to the amount of money I would have needed to cover things like bills, my receiving zakat al-fitr in the form of food was infinitely more beneficial than had I been given the same amount in money. The fact that it was food meant that I did not have to worry about going hungry for an entire six months. Had I been given it in money, it would have likely been used up in a matter of weeks.

> "It is preferable to pay before leaving the `Id prayer area, yet valid if one pays it beforehand or afterwards..."

- As the commentator mentions, means that zakat al-fitr is due until it is paid and the obligation does not expire with time. So even if one forgot to pay zakat al-fitr 20 years ago, it should be paid as soon as you remember and you are actually not sinful for delaying it, especially if it was done forgetfully.

Mukhtar li al-Fatawa's Chapter on Zakat[4]

Zakat is only incumbent upon a free, sane, adult Muslim...

Zakat is not due on slaves. Also non-Muslims do not pay zakat. What about jizya? It is simple: Muslims pay zakat and non-Muslims pay jizya in a Muslim state. Likewise, someone who is not of legal capacity does not pay zakat – *i.e.*, children do not pay zakat, nor do the mentally handicapped or insane. If a child has wealth (either through inheritance or money being saved by the parents in their name), there is no zakat upon it until they come of age. So when is it due?

If they possess a zakatable minimum (nisab) beyond their personal needs (hawa'ij asliyya) and their debts – with full ownership – at both the beginning and end of the zakat year (hawl).

Zakat is due if: (a) one possesses the nisab; (b) above-and-beyond their debts and immediate needs; (c) with complete possession. Zakat is only due on certain types of wealth, so the nisab is only considered on those types of wealth. In general, it is those types of wealth that are considered to have the meaning of nama (increase). Generally speaking, there is no zakat on personal belongings (*e.g.*, houses, cars, computers, clothing, electronics, *etc.*) Why? Because these matters are not considered in themselves to have the meaning of increase. They do not add to one's wealth, even though they may be included conventionally in one's "assets" in a court of law. Rather, zakat is due on things like paper money, bank accounts, stocks, investments, business inventory, *etc.*. All of these things have the "meaning" of increase in them since they are considered "wealth" and not personal property.

You must also possess it (*i.e.*, the zakatable item) with complete possession. This excludes lost items. If you, for instance, had ten gold bars and in travelling through the Gobi desert, lost it and launched an expedition to recover it – because it is not in your hand or accessible at the moment zakat is due, it is not considered.

It is not valid to give zakat except with an intention either at the time of putting aside the amount due or at the time of payment.

---

[4] For the purpose of this section, the bold text is a translation of Imam Mawsili's text and the regular font is our own commentary. And since we have already covered the basics of zakat, we will only reference the lines from Imam Mawsili's text which are needed to fill in the gaps which *Maraqi al-Sada`at* directed you to take from more detailed sources. We have also started at the beginning, since Imam Mawsili gives slightly more details than what was provided in *Maraqi al-Sa`adat*.

FIQH 112: ALMSGIVING (ZAKAT)

Zakat has to have intention: either at the time of giving or when putting aside the desired amount.

There is no zakat due on lost wealth.

Wealth that is lost is of two types. There is wealth that is lost even though there are reasonable ways of retrieving it and this is zakatable. For example, if one had a small backyard and one was sure that one lost some jewelry there, until one looked for it extensively, zakat would still be due upon it.[5] The other type is wealth that is lost without any reasonable means or expectation of retrieval. For example, if one lost wealth in the sea, for instance, or one did not know where it was lost, zakat is not due upon it. These are the two basic categories. There are are other sub-categories of lost wealth - but detailing them is beyond what we need at this time.

Zakat is due on wealth acquired [during the zakat year] and it is paid with the original wealth.

What does this refer to? Money acquired during the zakat year (whether through gift, inheritance, or other means) is counted with one's zakatable wealth. Zakat is due on the amount one possesses at the end of the zakat year – regardless of when it was required. There are therefore two dates to be considered: (a) once you possess your zakatable minimum, above and beyond debts and immediate expenses, your zakat year begins; (b) a year later, you look again and if you possess the zakatable minimum above and beyond your immediate expenses, zakat is due on what you currently have. If you do not have this zakatable minimum, there is no zakat due upon you.

What is zakat due upon? It is due upon all zakatable wealth you possess on that date, regardless of when it was acquired. Zakat is due on the wealth one had the entire year and the wealth that came in since then. It is a snapshot, like Western income taxes. Anything that is taxable is taxed, regardless of when it was acquired.

Zakat is due on the nisab-amounts, not amounts in-between.

This refers to zakatable situations like sheep: when there is an amount between two nisab thresholds, zakat is not due upon them – according to Imam Abu Hanifa. However, since most of us will likely only pay zakat on monetary items during our lifetime, this will probably not be an issue for anyone reading this.

Zakat is lifted if the zakatable amount is destroyed after it becomes due. If the amount is partially destroyed, then it is partially lifted.

If one's zakatable wealth is destroyed after zakat is due, the zakat is lifted from it. If some of it is destroyed, then it is lifted to the extent of what was destroyed. If twenty percent was destroyed, then your zakat is reduced by twenty percent. If one had a business inventory and zakat was due upon it by the 12th

---

[5] In our times, this would also apply to money that was stolen, but which is likely to be re-imbursed.

of Rajab, but it got destroyed on the 15th of Rajab, no zakat is due upon it (since it is not sinful to have a slight delay in zakat payment). Similarly, if zakat was due upon gold (or money) that was stolen, zakat would be lifted to the extent of what was stolen. However, this is if the wealth was destroyed or lost – not if it was used. If one had $50,000 in cash and spent it, zakat is still due since you were obliged to pay your zakat as soon as it was due. If you happened to have been negligent and spent that money on something else, your purchase does not lift your responsibility. And this is different from money that is stolen because the fact that it was stolen was beyond your control and so you are not held accountable. So how do you pay zakat?

Zakat is valid to pay in monetary value (qima).

If one had two sheep due in zakatable livestock, you do not have to actually pay two sheep, but you can pay their monetary value. If you have zakat due on your gold, since what is due is 2.5% of the weight value, you are permitted to pay it either in the gold itself or its monetary value.[6] You can also pay it in kind. If you are a businessman and zakat is due on inventory, you can give 2.5% of your inventory or something whose market value is the same as the amount that was due. So for example, if you purchased an iMac for $2,000 and zakat is due, you can give your iMac as zakat if its current market value is equal-to or above the monetary amount due upon you. But who do you give it to? To a poor Muslim. However, you have to do to at the current market value and in assessing its current value you should veer on the side of caution. You also should consider if a poor person really needs a 25" 2.5 Ghz iMac. Nonetheless, it can be given. Sometimes it is very useful to do this (*i.e.*, giving your iMac away as zakat to a struggling student for example) and that is why it has been mentioned. In such cases, what is considered is the current market value, not what you paid for it.

It is valid to pay zakat before it is due – whether for one or more years – if someone possesses the zakatable minimum.

You can pay zakat before it is due in that year. If it is due on the 10th of Rajab, you can pay it months ahead of time, as long as you make sure you pay what was due upon you, it is valid. If you preemptively gave $2,200 for example, and the actual time came around, you should make a mental note of the amount you have already paid and ensure that you gave the proper minimum amount. You can not only do this for this year, but for the next year, the year after, *etc.* You should just make sure that you keep a record and when the time actually comes that it is due, that at least the minimum amount had been paid.

Let's say you had members of your family who were struggling due to the man of the house getting laid off and you have the cash flow at the moment to assist them. You can give them money and consider it to be future zakat as long as you make sure you pay at least the amount due upon you. This is valid, as it is related from the Prophet (Allah bless him and give him peace) that he took two years worth of zakat from Abbas (may Allah be well pleased with him).

---

[6] For instance, if the gold a woman has was a gift from her grandmother, she would not have to give away her grandmother's gift. Instead, she could just have the amount of gold that is in the jewelry weighed and add the value of that gold to her zakatable amount.

FIQH 112: ALMSGIVING (ZAKAT)

What about delaying zakat payment? Zakat is due the instant the zakat year passes, however, it is recommended to pay it as soon as possible, improper to delay payment unnecessarily and sinful to delay it negligently. This means that a slight delay in paying it is fine, though it may be better to put aside immediately so that you do not accidentally spend it. Ibn `Abidin's conclusion on this matter is that negligent delay means delaying your zakat until the next zakat year begins. This is sinful. A delay without excuse is improper. A delay with excuse is acceptable (*e.g.*, you had bills you wanted to take care of and had the resolve to pay zakat at the beginning of next month), although it is best to pay as soon as one can.

LIVESTOCK

In terms of zakat on livestock, instead of translating the text which just provides the ratios, we will instead provide a table that gives the amounts in order to make it easier on both of us.

# of Camels	Zakat Due
1-5	N/A
6-9	1 goat
10-14	2 goats
15-19	3 goats
20-24	4 goats[7]
25-35	1 one year-old she-camel
36-45	1 two year-old she-camel
46-60	1 three year-old she-camel
61-75	1 four year-old she-camel
76-90	2 two year-old she-camels
91-120	2 three year-old she-camels
# of Goats/Sheep	Zakat Due
1-39	N/A
40-120	1 goat
121-200	2 goat

---

[7] *I.e.*, if you have less than 25 camels, you pay your zakat of them in goats since goats grow much quicker and are easier to feed and raise.

FIQH 112: ALMSGIVING (ZAKAT)

201-399	3 goats
400-499	4 goats
500-599	5 goats
Every 100 Additional	Add 1 more goat
# of Cattle (*i.e.*, cows or buffalo)[8]	**Zakat Due**
1-29	N/A
30-39	1 one year-old calf
40-59	1 two year-old calf
60-69	2 one year-old calves
70-79	1 one year-old and 1 two year-old calf
80-89	2 two year-old calves
90-99	3 one year-old calves

If you reflect upon these numbers, the amount that is paid upon cattle is an insignificant amount - especially compared to modern tax rates.

GOLD & SILVER

Zakat is due on both the minted and raw gold (thibr) and silver, as well as any jewelry or ornaments made from them – irrespective of whether one intended trade or not – if they reach the zakatable minimum (nisab).

The basis of zakat on gold and silver is that Allah has made them not only objects valued by humans, but they are considered to be money – *i.e.*, people have taken them as measures of wealth throughout history by Divine inspiration. They are stores of wealth.[9] This necessitates many things, the most important of which for our purposes is: zakat is taken on gold and silver, even if they are not being used as currency. If gold is in any other form, even those that are not used as a status of wealth (*e.g.*, decoration, jewelry, *etc.*), zakat is due upon it. Therefore money in the Shari`a is of two types: (1) things Allah has created intrinsically as measures of value (*i.e.*, those things innately considered money) and (2) those things

---

[8] Unlike camels, when dealing with cattle, there is no consideration to the sex of the animal being used to pay.
[9] This remains the case even in our time. Though gold "investment" is not considered to be lucrative, that is because it does not see a high return and instead functions more like a savings account. *I.e.*, "a store of wealth".

which are considered to be money through convention (*e.g.*, paper money in our times). Zakat is due upon the latter as well and the rulings of riba` apply.[10]

Thibr is raw gold prior to it being formed into anything. This is merely said to assert that zakat is due on gold and silver in all their forms. Normally, zakat is only due on possessions if one has the primary intention of trading with them. This is not the case with gold and silver. Zakat is due on them regardless of intention of their original acquisition, as long as their value reaches the nisab. The Qur'anic verses and ahadith are clear on this (as elucidated in *al-Ikhtiyar*).[11]

In terms of the zakatable minimum, their value is assessed and the nisab is established based upon their combined value. This applies to all zakatable assets: they are taken together to determine one's wealth from the zakatable items whose combined monetary value reaches the nisab. The nisab of gold is 20 mithqals, on which half a mithqal is due. Then in each four mithqals, two qirats are due. The nisab of silver is 200 dirham, on which five dirhams are due. Then, in each 40 dirhams, one dirham is due. This is the classical measurement, but in our times we know the zakatable minimum by gram weight. Our scholars have exerted much effort in order to determine the accurate equivalent measures so that people can determine things like zakat (as well as travel) without difficulty.[12]

The zakatable minimum that corresponds to al-Mawsili's statement is 87.5 grams and 2.5% is due upon this. You do not only give zakat on your gold if it reaches the zakatable minimum on its own. Rather: (a) there is one zakatable minimum and all the zakatable wealth is considered by its monetary value, if it all reaches the nisab collectively, zakat is due their combined value; (b) you do not pay zakat <u>on the monetary value</u> of the gold items that you have; instead, you pay zakat according to the <u>weight value</u> of the gold in the jewelry or the other gold items in your possession.

For example, if you had an heirloom gold necklace worth $20,000 as a result of the age, craftmanship and other jewels it contains, you do not pay zakat upon this total value. Rather, you pay zakat upon the weight value of the gold that the necklace contains. How does one determine this? You should take it to a jeweler in order to determine how many grams of gold it actually contains and pay zakat upon that according to its weight. What about gold in which other things are mixed? The predominant state is considered. So if

---

[10] This is important to state because there are some people who push the idea that zakat is not due on paper money because it has no intrinsic value. Though there are complications with paper money that should definitely be considered, the reliable fatwa of all Four Canonical Schools is that zakat is due upon conventional forms of money as well.

[11] The detailed proof of this is beyond our level and the Ikhtiyar of Imam Mawsili is considered to be an advanced text in the Hanafi School. But as I said earlier in the chapter, proof that jewellry is a form of wealth is demonstrated in the fact that the female Companions used it to pay their zakat and give charity when requested. Among the numerous hadith narrations that the Hanafi School cites as proof is the following, "`A'ishah (may Allah be pleased with her) said, 'The Messenger of Allah (may Allah bless him and give him peace) entered upon me and saw band rings of silver on my hand. He said, "What is this, O `A'ishah?!" I replied, "I put them on to make myself beautiful for you, O Messenger of Allah!" He said, "Do you pay their zakat?" I said, "No." He said, "They are sufficient for you [as a share] of the Fire [of Hell].'" (Abu Dawud)

[12] That is to say, how they arrived at that number is too complicated to explain here. But the scholars are in general agreement over these measurements.

something is predominantly base metals, then it is considered like commodities are and if the silver or gold predominate, then they are considered silver or gold.

I.e., if something has less than 50% gold, it is considered like a trade item and you give zakat based upon the rules regulating zakat upon commodities.[13] This is because gold and silver are rarely free of some amount of metals which are mixed in them due to their soft natural state. A small amount of metals being mixed with them is ignored. But if something is predominately other than gold or silver, you only pay zakat upon them if their primary purpose was trade. There is no zakat on commodities unless they are for trade and their monetary value reaches the zakatable minimum of either gold or silver. The value of trade goods is added to that of gold and silver in determining the nisab. If one had a car, for example, and one was thinking about selling it – it is not a tradable good by virtue of that fact. Instead once it is actually set aside and put up for sale, it then becomes a tradable good (based upon its market value).

If one is a businessman, one needs to learn the fiqh of zakat for trade, as there are many considerations that need to be understood which are not explained in general primers, such as: the evaluation of one's inventory, old/unsold inventory, *etc*. Sometimes, people have very large inventories and the zakat due upon it could potentially be very high were the general principles elucidated here applied and so the scholars took that into consideration and passed judgements about it.

Since gold and silver are no longer the primary currency, our scholars have set the zakatable minimum at the amount of gold one would have to own for zakat to have been deemed obligatory in the past. Based upon this, if you go by the gold standard, the zakatable minimum (nisab) is currently approximately $3,700 and $331 based on the silver standard. However, since the value of silver is so low, many scholars have given the opinion that zakat is due based upon the gold standard. Therefore, if you combine the value of your zakatable assets and they reach $3,700, you wait an entire year, revalue your assets and pay 2.5% if it remains over that minimum amount.

CROPS & FRUIT

A tenth (10%) is due on anything watered by rainfall or its runoff, whether the output is a little or a lot – except for qasab farisi, wood, and grass.

I.e., in agricultural produce, there is no zakatable minimum. Rather, the consideration is whether or not one's crops were watered naturally (by rain or the direction consequence of it) and if that is the case then a tenth is due, except for the things mentioned. Qasab farisi is cane. These three things (cane, wood and grass) are things that are not ordinarily sought out from the ground as agricultural produce. However, if the ground is specifically prepared for the gathering of cane, wood or grass, a tenth would be due from it. I.e., if one had a timber farm, then the zakat would be due on it since the trees are being raised in order to turn to wood and sell.

---

[13] *I.e.*, if it is primarily composed of platinum, but has been mixed with silver and was purchased for trade, its market value is taken and not the weight of the silver it contains. However, if it is purchased for personal use, it is not considered in one's zakat since it is considered platinum jewelry, not stored silver

Half a tenth (5%) is due on anything watered by water-wheels or watermills. There is nothing due on straw or palm branches.

I.e., when watering is done through human intervention, 5% is due since there are greater costs in producing such crops for the farmer. Straw and palm branches are excluded since they are by-products which are not sought in-and-of-themselves. So zakat would be due on the dates, but not the palm leaves, even if they are sold to make fiber. The same applies to other crops where the by-products are not the reason the crop is being grown.

Costs and maintenance aren't deducted before the zakat that is due on crops.
Costs associated with agricultural produce is due on the entire output and not the net output once costs are subtracted. That is, zakat is due upon the gross amount and not the net amount. The associated costs are upon the farmer. The Prophet (Allah bless him and give him peace) imposed zakat on the output with no consideration for the costs of production or maintenance.

There is no zakat on that which is extracted from the seas, such as pearls, amber, and marjan. There is no zakat on that which is found in mountains, such as gypsum or limestone, or yaqut, fayruzaj, or zurmud.

Yaqut, fayruzaj and zurmud are the names of different precious stones extracted from the earth. Zakat is not taken from them due to the lack of textual evidence. However, once they become tradeable commodities, zakat is due upon them as tradeable items – if one has diamonds, rubies, pearls, *etc*., as personal possessions, zakat is not due upon them. So in general, no tax is owed for the possession of mines. Zakat is only due for mined products once they have been extracted, polished and readied for sale. Then, they are treated as commodities and not like gold or silver. Gold and silver are the only to precious substances which are intrinsically considered to be wealth.

The Greater Pilgrimage (Hajj)

As with the previous chapter, we will only comment upon the most important points since this is not practical. Even those who have performed the Hajj always refresh their knowledge of it as a part of their preparations once they have formalized their trip. More than anything act of worship, since this is only performed once or twice (since many people wind up doing both an Umra and a Hajj), it is pretty much guaranteed that you are not going to remember the details of this chapter (unless you have them memorized) and will necessarily have to review it once it becomes relevant in the future.

Also, since Hajj is something that needs to be experienced, we do not believe that diagramming anything to help you memorize any of the rulings will be particularly helpful. Prior to you going, you will more than likely be given a "crash course" if you attend with a Hajj travel group. At that time, you should review the fiqh that is mentioned in Maraqi al-Sada`at, since the people hosting many not necessarily follow the Hanafi School. What will be more beneficial for you at this time is to perhaps collect the various Arabic du'as and adhkar that should be said at the various stages of the trip and make your own dhikr pamphlet to help you recite the adhkar and du'as that should be said at each phase of the ritual. This, in fact, can (and perhaps should) be included in your assignment for this chapter..

"Hajj is defined as visit a particular place…"
- This is obviously in reference to Makka and is not valid to any other place. The author is giving the linguistic definition, which is usually followed by the a more specific shari☐ definition, but perhaps declined to do since this is an abbreviated text.

"And as soon as one is able to…"
- Meaning that as soon as one has the money and ability to perform Hajj, doing so is obligatory. If one has the money and not the ability or has the ability and not the money, it is not obligatory. Once both conditions are met, it becomes obligatory and remains so until performed. The point at which this is actually the case is discussed in the next paragraph.

"The obligatory requirements for its performance are…"
- "A sound and healthy body…571. This same ruling would apply to being wrongfully imprisoned". In the event that someone has been wrongfully by an unjust ruler (or framed by another person for a crime they did not commit, for example), if they had otherwise met the conditions for Hajj, then they are permitted to pay for and designate another individual to perform Hajj on their behalf in order to discharge the obligation. However, if someone was actually guilty of the crime, they are obliged to wait until they are released. As for the case of someone who may have committed a crime, but converted while in prison, we are seeking a fatwa on this issue. However, due to the cost of Hajj in our times, it is unlikely that this would apply to many people.
- "And to be accompanied by her husband or unmarriageable kin…" is the relied upon position in the Hanafi School. So, if a woman is unmarried or cannot find a mahram to take her, the obligation of performing the Hajj herself is lifted and she would be obliged to designate someone to perform it on her behalf. However, there are some Hanafi scholars in contemporary times that have permitted women to

perform Hajj without their husband or unmarriageable male relatives if they are accompanying close female family who have either their husbands or mahrams present. It would not be permitted for a woman to perform Hajj with a group that does not include close female relative and their husbands, sons or uncles, *etc.*, in the Hanafi school. This is as long as it is their obligatory Hajj. If they have already performed Hajj in the past as adults, then the original ruling remains.

HOW TO PERFORM THE RITES OF HAJJ

NOTE: **We have included a Hajj Guide so that you can see the steps of Hajj in pictures. Please review it as you are reviewing this chapter to get a better grasp on the steps of Hajj and Umra.**

"When one intends to enter the state of pilgrim sanctity at one of the designated boundaries…"

- The ihram listed is for men. As for women, they wear their normal clothing, minus the gloves and face veil (for those who wear them out of religious precaution).[1] As for the miqat, they are essential to know, but if you are going directly to Hajj, an announcement is made on the airplane when you are approaching the miqat which applies to you so that the men can change into their ihram before crossing the boundary.

---

[1] Whether or not the niqab and gloves are valid is a contentious issue in our times. The face, hands and feet are not considered to be awrah in the Hanafi School. However, earlier scholars considered it wajib for young women (i.e., those who are at ages when they are typically sought for marriage) to cover their face in the presence of men whom they are allowed to potentially marry out of the consideration of reducing sexual tensions in the public sphere. However, cultural norms of clothing have changed so much in the last 10 years alone that many scholars have argued that it is more important for women to properly cover those aspects of her body that are considered to be nakedness and insisting upon her covering her face is like preparing food for a drowning man. The fact that he may very well be hungry is besides the point and is a misplaced priority. Similarly, in a time where most women in Western societies walk around in skin tight clothing and frequently expose the majority of their bodies in public, insisting that Muslim women are a source of "fitna" for not covering their face is pretty hard to argue. Instead, what women in our time should focus on is making sure that their clothing is loose, their bust (*i.e.*, head, neck and cleavage line) is properly covered and they avoid wearing makeup and perfume while in public. What we have seen from our scholars is that they only insist on the niqab in religious settings when young men and women will be in close proximity of each other or if they move to Muslim countries where women wearing face veils in public is the societal norm. Otherwise, insisting that she wear a face veil to work or when she is going to the Masjid is not necessary (unless she is attending a Masjid which may have this as policy and would prevent her from entering without one), especially when the unfortunate reality of our times is that most women in the Muslim World do not wear hijab to begin with. The fact that none of the Four Canonical Schools consider it permissible for a woman to wear niqab while in ihram is explicit proof that it is not from her awrah and covering her face is therefore based upon secondary considerations. Even the Prophet's wives (may Allah be well pleased with them), who were obligated to cover their faces by consensus, did not do so while performing Hajj and instead only temporarily pulled their hijab over their faces when non-mahram men happened to approach them. In a situation where a woman knows that a particular man is attracted to her, she should avoid them as best as she can and limit her interactions to that which is absolutely necessary, while ensuring that she does nothing that could be misinterpreted as flirtatious. (The same also applies to men when they know that a particular woman is attracted to them as well.) This is the upshot of the situation. More details are mentioned in "ADAB 102: Prohibitions of the Tongue" for those who have not yet taking that course.

FIQH 112: THE GREATER PILGRIMAGE (HAJJ)

Likewise, if you are visiting the Prophet (Allah bless him and give him peace) prior to attending the Hajj,[2] then you will be told about the miqat as you are driving on the bus on the way to perform it.

"If, rather, he is performing tamattu'..."
- There are actually three ways to perform Hajj: tamattu', qiran and ifrad. Hajj tamattu' is when you perform Umra and then transition into Hajj. Hajj qiran is when you simultaneously intend Hajj and Umra at the same time (similar to how wudu can be intended while performing ghusl). Hajj ifrad is when you perform Hajj "in isolation": *i.e.*, you perform Hajj with absolutely no intention on performing Umra. The reason why the first two would be done is that performing Hajj is an obligation, while performing Umra is a sunna and standing recommendation. Since it is difficult for people to make it to Makka, many prefer performing both Hajj and Umra while they are there since it is not guaranteed that they will be able to afford another trip to Makka in the future. Tamattu' in particular allows the individual to do the things that are prohibited for Hajj and Umra during the short gap which exists between the two. Otherwise, if one wanted to perform Umra after or before Hajj in a way that makes them completely separate, you would have to leave the vicinity of Makka after completing your Hajj or Umra and the re-enter your ihram from the miqat you left from. There is scholarly disagreement over which is preferred, but that level of detail, you will discover when you are actually preparing to perform the Hajj and need to decide which of them is possible for you to do in the particular package that you have signed up for.

"At this point, the pilgrim must abstain…"
- "Sexual intercourse or speaking about it in front of women…" in ways that are permissible, such as if medical advice is being sought or fiqh is being discussed. Hajj/Umra is not the time or place for such conversations. Otherwise, speaking about the act of sexual intercourse in front of women (or women in front of men) is unlawful and is considered vulgarity.
- "Vulgar speech, Argumentation, Acts of disobedience…" are all haram anyway, but are even more haram when one is in ihram, just as they are even more haram when one is fasting. What each of these entails are discussed in "ADAB 102: Prohibitions of the Tongue".
- "Covering the head or the face…" *i.e.*, to keep from getting overheated. As for covering the face for "fitna", we have discussed that in the first footnote above. And it is generally makruh for men to cover their face in any situation unless there is a specific need to do so (*e.g.*, protect themselves from the cold, sandstorms or as safety precaution in one's profession).
- "Applying any sort of scent…" that is after you initially put on perfume after you ghusl for ihram. And this applies to men. Women wearing any perfume (whether it be actual perfume or heavily scented lotions and creams) is not permissible in public. During ihram, men should also avoid using scented soaps, lotions or hair gels, as these things would be considered applying scents.
- "One should recite much talbiya… with a raised voice" for men. Women generally should not raise their voice in the presence of non-mahram men, though her voice slightly out of earshot is acceptable. Again, the details of this are mentioned in ADAB 102.

---

[2] Unfortunately, this has been made an issue in the last 100 years or so, due to the promotion and spread of opinions related to this that were considered to be aberrant and mistaken in the past. Visiting the Prophet (Allah bless him and give him peace) is not an unlawful bid`a and actually was considered to be recommended by consensus in the past - the one or two opinions which violated this consensus were ignored. We will return to this issue again when we reach the end of this chapter.

"Supplication is accepted upon seeing the Ennobled House…"

- And looking at the Ka'aba while in prayer is permissible in the Hanafi School. Doing so is actually recommended in other Schools, but the Hanafis reason that those who are not used to looking directly ahead may get easily distracted. But unlike other times, doing so neither makruh nor considered to be khilaf al-awla. However, since the congregation is often mixed while at the Haram Sharif due to women constantly performing tawaf, if you looking directly ahead will cause you to stare at a woman (or a woman start at man who may be attractive to her), then you should look down at the point of prostration as you normally do.

"He should then face the Black Stone … and kiss it, without harming anyone." Since the Ka'aba is so crowded and there are people constantly moving, trying to touch the Black Stone, there is a little bit of roughness that is expected. Our American culture is one that expects a lot more personal space than most other societies and so strangers touching, bumping or even pushing you is something that you will have to get used to and keep yourself from not getting angry over. If you happen to be someone who suffers from claustrophobia, germ-related OCD and explosive disorder, you should perhaps refrain from trying to make tawaf close to the Ka'aba. Otherwise, it is okay for you to slowly force your way towards the Black Stone as you are circling the Ka'aba without knocking people over. But do not try to walk straight towards it while people are performing tawaf, which will probably be impossible anyway. If you are accompanying women or elderly individuals though, you have to take them into consideration and perhaps try to kiss the Black Stone on a different occasion since it may be dangerous for them if they are small or do not have the strength to resist against the force of the crowd.

"He should then perform tawaf"

- Which, outside of Hajj and Umra, is recommended to do as much as you can since the Prophet (Allah bless him and give him peace) said "Tawaf around the House is like prayer, except that you may speak during it. So whoever speaks during it, let him not speak of anything but what is good."[3] (Tirmidhi) However, other things (like jogging between Safa and Marwa) are only to be done by those performing Hajj or Umra.
- "If performing Hajj alone, he should intention the Tawaf of Arrival" which takes the place of the two raka's of Tahiyyat al-Masjid for the one who does not live in Makka.
- While the description of tawaf and the other rites of Hajj may seem complicated or difficult to follow, when you are there, everyone else will be doing them, so it will come natural. For the moment, try to focus more on the things which invalidate the Hajj, as well as what is recommended and the like, instead of focusing too much on something that will make a lot more sense when you are actually there yourself. However, imaging yourself doing it also helps you learn and in many places, Hajj "seminars" include trying to replicate the rites as though you are doing them - which also is a good practice to do after you have gone through the basic fiqh.

"He then performs two raka's of prayer behind the Station of Ibrahim"

---

[3] Since tawaf is not something that is a part of the religious practices of Westerners, it would be good for everyone to look up the virtues of tawaf when they have the time, since the idea of "walking" as an act of worship is foreign to our religious culture. This would include the adhkar (plural of dhikr) that are recommended to be done by the one performing tawaf, since these adhkar will help "give life" to the act.

- Which is marked in the Haram Sharif a smaller gold structure that is hard to miss. During Hajj, you will a crowd of people walking towards it after doing their tawaf, so you can just follow them if you are unsure where it is.
- "He next proceeds to Mount Safa [which he ascends]..."
- Though it is referred to as "Mount Safa" and "Mount Marwa" they are more like hills than mountains. As you walk the distance, there will be a gradual incline which will dramatically increase when you get to the end of the "track". Men in particular are encouraged to walk on the steeper part of it, while women should walk at a slower pace and not over exert themselves. This is especially true in our time, since the entire area is covered by ceramic tile, which makes jogging on it while barefoot particularly hard on the knees. But the tile keeps the area clean, which otherwise would be full of dust and very difficult to maintain.

"He combines these two prayers, praying them both it he time of zuhr..."
- <u>This is the only time in which combining prayers outside of its time is permitted in the Hanafi School.</u> Though this opinion is not common overall, it can easily be argued to be the strongest from the standpoint of evidence. In the ahadith, which the Companions mention the fact that the Prophet (Allah bless him and give him peace) "joined" the prayer, it can either mean that he prayed one in the time of another or that he delayed one prayer until the end of its time and then immediately prayed the next one. That he did the latter and not the former was observed to the practice of the Companions by the Followers and the interpretation of the Prophet's (Allah bless him and give him peace) joining given by many Companions in the hadith collections. Among the narrations which support this, is the fact that our Mother `A'isha (may Allah be well pleased with her) said "The Messenger of Allah (Allah bless him and give him peace) on a journey would delay Zuhr and bring `Asr forward and delay Maghrib and bring Isha forward." (Ahmad, Tahawi, Hakim) One of the best contemporary treatments of this issue was done by Mawlana Zafar Ahmad al-Uthmani in his wonderful *I'la al-Sunna* in which he demonstrates that the opinion that the Prophet (Allah bless him and give him peace) did not literally join any prayer outside of the Hajj is the only opinion which harmonizes all of the authentic hadith that have been narrated about this issue. Fortunately, this chapter has been translated, since it is a common criticism of would-be hadith scholars in places like Pakistan. In it, he demonstrates that while the Hanafis are frequently criticized for sticking to this position, it is perhaps the one which makes the most sense and does not rely on a superficial reading of the hadith, which ignoring the narrations while contradict such an interpretation.[4]

---

[4] We are not meaning to disrespect or undermine the acceptable positions of any of the Four Canonical Schools. We accept that the Shafi`i and Hanbali position is valid. However, many people are influenced to contradict the positions of their imams on the grounds that the "evidence against it is stronger" by people who often have not bothered to research the legal reasoning of the other opinion. In this case, some Shafi`i scholars admit that their position on this issue is probably the weakest in the entire Shafi`i School for the very reason that it relies on a superficial reading of a few hadith, while ignoring other evidence against argues against this interpretation. For that reason, a number of Shafi`is scholars we know have adopted the practice of joining the prayer in the time of the first and then repeating the second in its proper time in order to remove the difference of opinion over the validity of literal joining. So let no one who follows the Hanafi School think that their opinion on this "contradicts the hadith" and be pressured into do something that contradicts the verified and well-researched conclusions of their Madhhab. The only time it is permitted to pray a prayer early is while one is on Arafa during Hajj and late while one is at Muzdalifa, since both of these times are the only times where it can be proven beyond a reasonable doubt that the Prophet (Allah bless him and give him peace) either prayed Asr in Zhuhr's time or prayed Maghrib during the time of `Isha.

FIQH 112: THE GREATER PILGRIMAGE (HAJJ)

"As sunrise approaches… He stones at the Jamrat al-Aqaba only… with each throw…"

- The "throw" mentioned here and in the footnotes is more like a "toss". It is a symbolic action and should not be done with a great deal of force. Unfortunately, you may find many people get overly excited and begin throwing larger stones or even shoes in their religious fervor. Though their enthusiasm may be heart warming, throwing large stones is potentially dangerous and nothing that we do in Hajj should put another person in harm's way.
- "He then shaves his head…" which was actually said out of order, perhaps by mistake, since our author mentions the sacrifice before shaving in both *Maraqi al-Falah* and *Imdad al-Fattah* - both of which are commentaries on *Nur al-Idah*. Please take note of what the commentator says in the footnote.[5]

"He then shaves his head or trims his hair…"

- This is for men. If you have hair, shave your head. Even if you have locks that you have been growing for 15 years, shave your head. Doing so is sunna and refraining for no reason is permissible, but refusing to shave your head for no legitimate reason goes against what is preferred (khilaf al-awla). Despite the fact that most of the Companions had long hair, they considered shaving their hair after Hajj and Umrah to be like a badge of honor. That remains the case in our times and the amount of respect and du'a you will get from people who realize that you have just returned from Hajj due to the condition of your scalp is perhaps reason enough to shave it fully. A valid reason not to "shave" your head would be if you are African-American and using a razor would cause you to break out in razor bumps. In that case, you should try to find an electric razor to shave your head with. Since we are the only group of people who have this problem, you may have to plan ahead for this or go to the barbers who offer this service with someone who speaks Arabic. Otherwise, the men who do the shaving there use a straight razor and they are not going to do with the same care as one of us would do back home since they do not have the same concerns as people of African descent do regarding develop a skin condition unless certain preparations are taken.

"He performs the two rak'as of tawaf and then goes to the area of Zamzam… He should take out the Zamzam by himself if he is able to do so"

- In the mid-2000s, direct access to the well of Zamzam was closed. Instead of drinking directly from the spouts that have been installed to draw water directly from the well, workers constantly bring cold and room temperature water. You will be given a cup to drink from and immediately throw away in the garbage. This is because the floor is marble and having it wet is very dangerous. So please comply with all of the rules and expectations that you are presented with. This includes trying to fill up large bottles of Zamzam water in order to take them back home. At the airport, you are allowed to purchase one jug of Zamzam per person, which last time I was there cost around $15. Trying to take more than this would weigh down the plane and make travel unsafe.

---

[5] And this is the more academically honest way of correcting a text. Unfortunately, book publishers in our times have the bad habit of "correcting" the original text, which sometimes mean that they are inserting their opinion over a matter that is disagreed upon in a way that hides the disagreement and makes the opinion that they are opposing seem invalid. We have given an example of this being done and the effect that it has had below with respect to the ziyara (visitation) of the Messenger of Allah (Allah bless him and give him peace).

FIQH 112: THE GREATER PILGRIMAGE (HAJJ)

"He then proceeds to the door of the Ka'ba and kisses its threshold…"

- This is again if you are able to without much difficulty or harming others. Since there are so many people now performing Hajj and Umra year round (al-hamdu li-Llah), you may only be able to do this early in the morning during tahajjud time. By the time the Fajr prayer is called, inner courtyard of the Haram Sharif is usually full and remains that way until very late or early the next morning.

"In all the rites of Hajj and `Umra, the woman does the same as the man except…"

- "She should not go in between a crowd of men when greeting the Black Stone…" which is not safe for women on their own, unfortunately, due to the men pushing their way to try to touch the Black Stone and wall of the Ka'ba. If she would like to touch the Black Stone, she should have her husband or adult son escort her, while he holds her hand and carves out a path for her in the crowd. Otherwise, there will be so many people there that she won't be able to make a path on her own and will wind up rubbing her body against the men around her due to the crowd concentration.

"Visiting the Prophet (Allah bless him and give him peace) is an emphasized sunna, either before or after the Hajj."

- This is unfortunately has become a controversial statement due to the adoption and promotion of an opinion of a particular scholar who opposed the consensus of everyone before him on this issue by the Saudi officials. In the appendices that follow the translation of our text, Faraz Khan has added the chapter on Visitation of the Messenger of Allah (Allah bless him and give him peace) from the *Ikhtiyar* of Imam Mawsili. For those of you who are not aware of who he is yet, Imam Mawsili is the "Shaykh al-Islam" of the Hanafi School. He was from Mosul, Iraq and was born about 30 years before Imam Nawawi. Therefore, he is considered to be from the middle period of Islamic scholarship which is frequently called "The Golden Age of Islam". Despite being a relatively "late" figure in comparison to figures like Imam Tahawi and Imam al-Quduri, his *Mukhtar li al-Fatawa ala Madhhab Imam al-A`dham Abu Hanifa al-Nu□man* is often considered to be one of the 6 "mother books" of the Hanafi School from which the most reliable opinions can be found. The *Ikhtiyar* from which this section was taken is Imam Mawsili's own commentary on this work and is considered to be a masterpiece, studied by advanced students in traditional institutions due to his incorporating usul al-fiqh and a bit of comparative fiqh throughout the work. What is the point of us mentioning all of this? This being in a work like *Al-Ikhtiyar* is proof enough that this opinion was standard at the time and was not controversial in the slightest. Imam Nawawi also includes in his *Kitab al-Adhkar* a section called "Visiting the Tomb of the Messenger of Allah and the Remembrances of Allah Made There"[6] in the chapter of Hajj in which he begins by saying

> Know that everyone who performs the hajj should set out to visit the Messenger of Allah (Allah bless him and give him peace), whether it is on one's way or not, for visiting him (Allah bless him and give him peace) is one of the most important acts of worship, the most rewarded of efforts, and best of goals.

Unfortunately, the current custodians of the Prophet's Mosque (Allah bless him and give him peace) oppose this and so you may not be able to implement all of the things mentioned by Imam Mawsili in the

---

[6] In the versions of Imam Nawawi's *Al-Adhkar* that have been printed in Saudi Arabia, this section has been changed to say "Visiting the Mosque of the Messenger of Allah" and edits have been made to everything Imam Nawawi recommended which contradicts the opinion of the muftis and scholars of Saudi Arabia.

appendix. For instance, you will not be allowed to stand in one place for more than a few seconds and you are prohibited from raising your hands in du'a since the guards present there will unfortunately interpret such actions as "praying to the Prophet" (Allah bless him and give him peace). The most you will be allowed to do is give your salams to the Prophet (Allah bless him and give him peace), Abu Bakr and Umar, say a very short du'a and exit the Masjid. If you bring anything to read in their presence in order to help you remember what to say, it will likely be confiscated or you will be pushed out of the Masjid.[7] In general, while you are in Makka and Madina, listen to the guards and save yourself from getting into unnecessary trouble. Unfortunately, women are no longer allowed to visit the Prophet (Allah bless him and give him peace) from the front or pray in the Rawda as the men do. Instead, there is a small section behind their resting places that you are expected to give you salams from and pray your two raka'as at. If you go on Hajj or Umra during a busy season, expect that this area will be crowded and so you will have to fight at least a little in order to pray your two raka'as and you are going to have to put up with getting pushed, elbowed or stepped on due to the limitations that have been placed on women visiting the Prophet (Allah bless him and give him peace) by the Saudi authorities who would perhaps forbid it completely if they could, but doing so is difficult since the Masjid had to be built around his resting place.

THE LESSER PILGRIMAGE (UMRA)

- Umra is much shorter than the Hajj and all of its rites are confined to the Masjid al-Haram. Many people, perform multiple Umras while they are in Makka, though some scholars considered this to be offensive. That is not the case for the Hanafi School. If you desire to perform more than one Umra, the only major difference the second time around would be that you should pass a razor over your head even though you shaved it the first time. You would also be required to leave the Haram and re-enter it before you can perform another valid Umra, though not so far that you leave the miqat.

EXPIATION (FIDYA) FOR VIOLATIONS

"The sacrifice of a sheep is mandatory as expiation for any one of the following…"
- "To wear a stitched garment…" applies to anything that is worn the usual way it is worn that supports one's clothing. The commentator mentions wearing a jacket over one's shoulders without putting your hands in the sleeves as an exception. Similar to this is wearing a "fanny pack" which many men wear in order to hold their money, hotel key and the things that they otherwise would not be able to hold as a result of being in the simple clothing required for ihram. If you wear a fanny pack, you should wear it under your upper garment so it does not potentially violate the condition of not wearing a stitched garment. If you wore it over your ihram clothing, it would function like a belt it and thus like a piece of

---

[7] I myself was prevented from continuing to read a work of salawat, even outside of the Masjid, while I was there in an attempt to implement the statement of Imam Mawsili "He then stands directed towards his face with his back toward the qibla and sends as many blessings upon him as he wishes" on the grounds that "Dhikr should be directed towards the Qibla and not the Prophet". So if you have the opportunity, do as much as you are allowed and then do everything else that has been recommended from the Masjid with the intention on it being a visitation of the Prophet (Allah bless him and give him peace) who is presented with the salawat that people make upon him and returns it by name to whomever does so according to the authentic ahadith on the matter.

clothing. If, however, it is being worn under the upper garment, it is not functioning as a piece of clothing and would there not violate this rule.

HUNTING VIOLATIONS

- We shall skip this section, since you will not be hunting and will be provided with food in your hotel.

This concludes our FIQH 112 Companion. While there are some sections we have skipped, we encourage you to still read the other sections so that you will be familiar with them if and when you are presented with the opportunity to study them from a qualified scholar. Also, please do not forget that Sh. Faraz Khan has given a wonderful appendix at the end of the official translation which provides all the supplications that were mentioned throughout the work in Arabic. You may want to go back and forth between this appendix and the sections of the book you are studying in order to see the supplications he has transliterated.

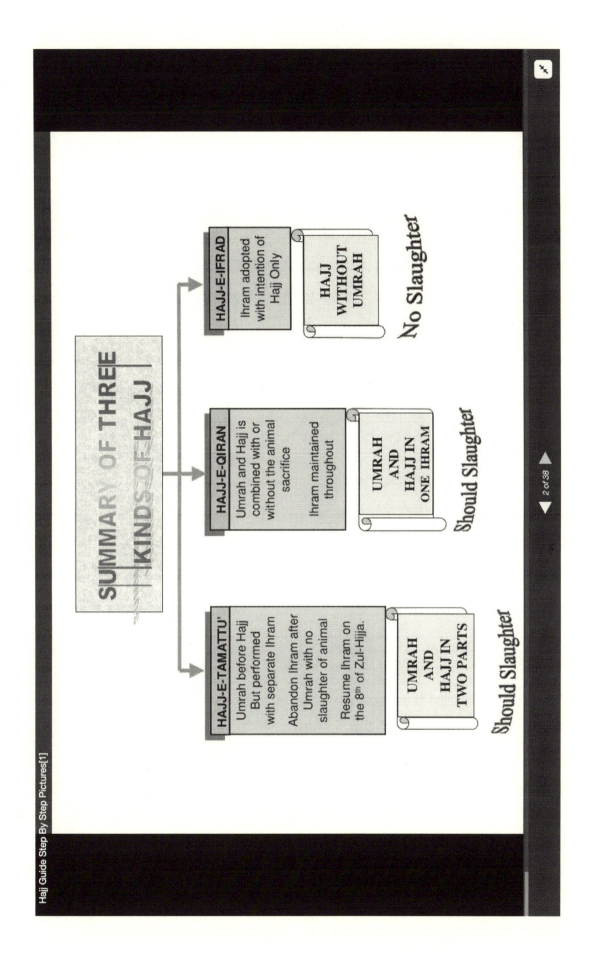

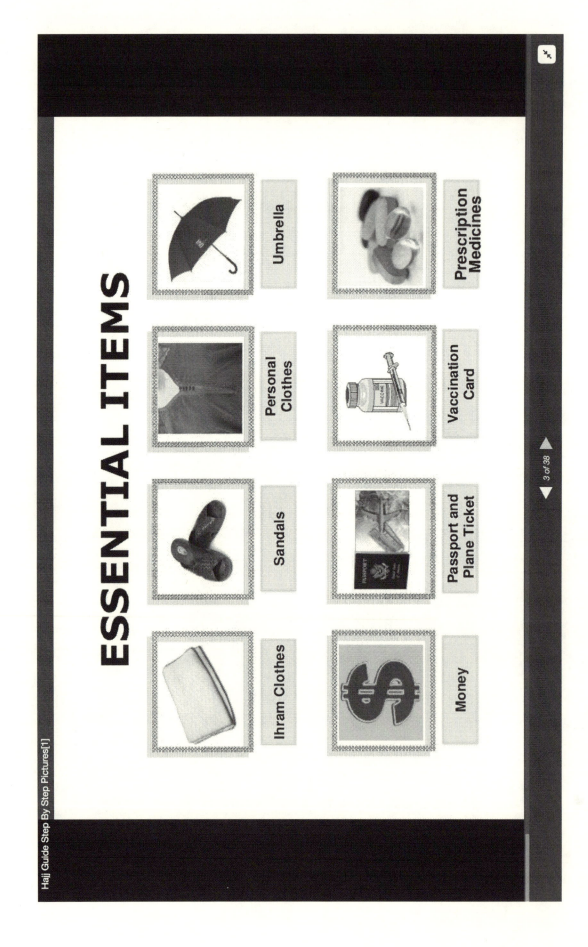

Men's Ihram

Ihram for men consists of two pieces of white, un sewn cloth, One of the piece (izar) is wrapped around the midriff to cover his body from just above his navel to his ankles, and the other (Rida) is draped around his shoulders to cover the upper body.

HAJJ PILGRIM WEARING IHRAM

Idtiba:

is practiced only while actually performing Tawaf ul Qudoom

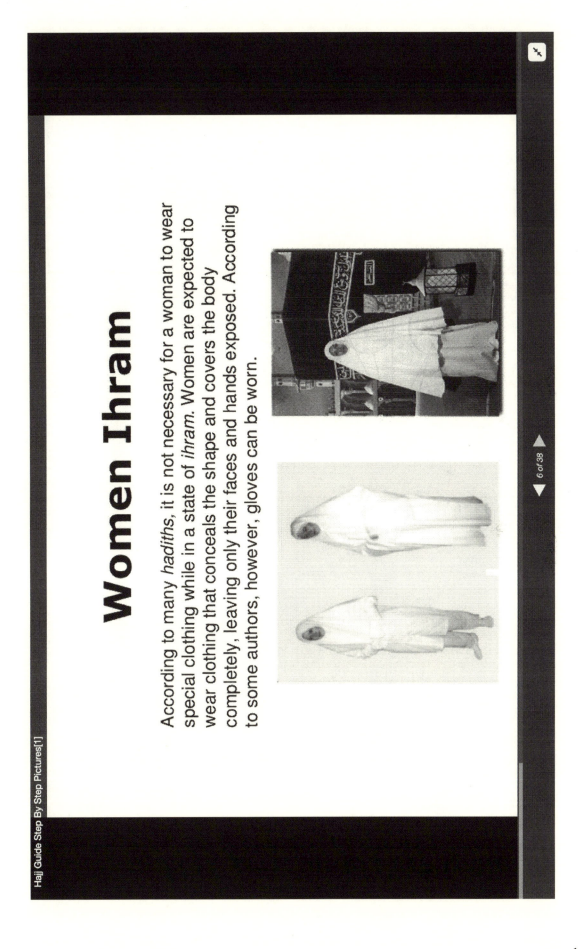

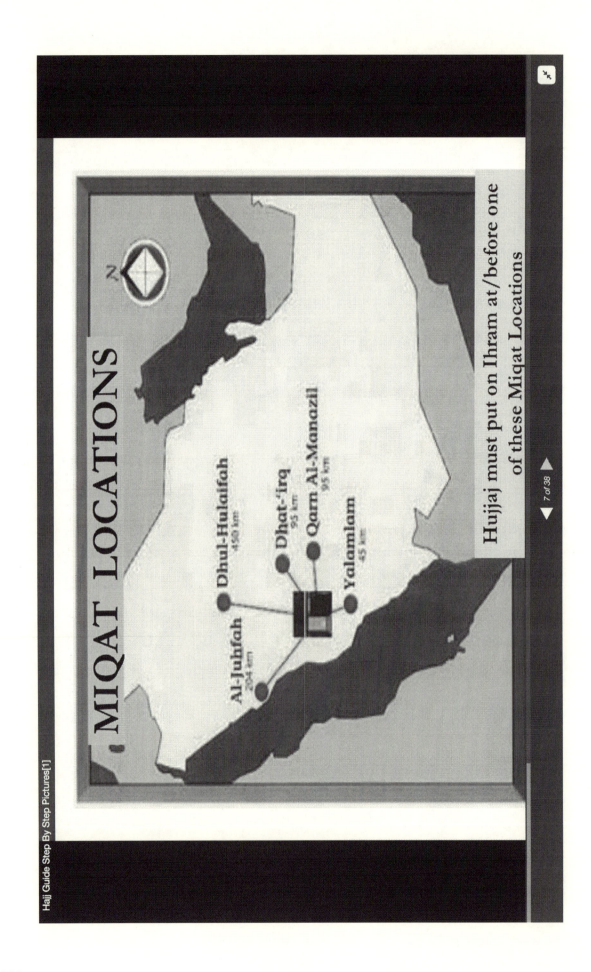

لَبَّيْكَ اللَّهُمَّ لَبَّيْكَ، لَبَّيْكَ لَا شَرِيكَ لَكَ لَبَّيْكَ، إِنَّ الْحَمْدَ وَالنِّعْمَةَ لَكَ وَالْمُلْكَ، لَا شَرِيكَ لَكَ

"Here I am, O Lord, here I am, You indeed have no partner, here I am.

No Doubt, all praise and bounties are yours, and so is the absolute Domain. You indeed have no partners, here I am"

Masjid Al-Haraam

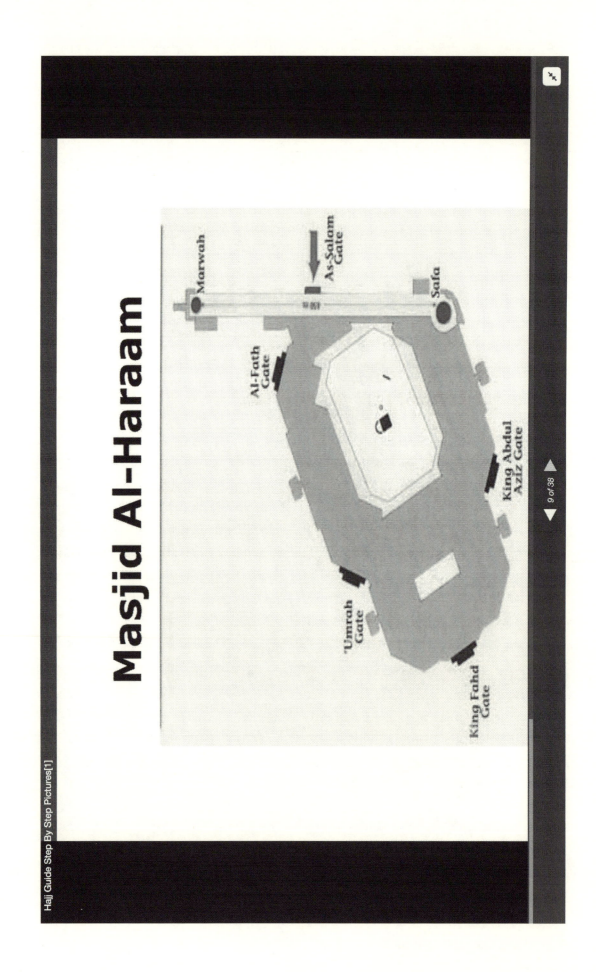

TYPE OF TAWAF

- **Tawaful Qudoom:**
  Initial Tawaf when pilgrims enter for the first time in the Masjid ul-Haram. This is the only time that requires Ihram with Idtiba (Leaving right armpits uncover)

- **Tawaful-Ifada:**
  Performed on the 10th of Thul Hijja – The first day of Eid

- **Tawaful-Wadaa:**
  Farewell Tawaf before leaving Makkah

- **Tawaful-Nafl:**
  Extra Tawaf that the pilgrims can perform at any time during their visit in Makkah with/without Ihram

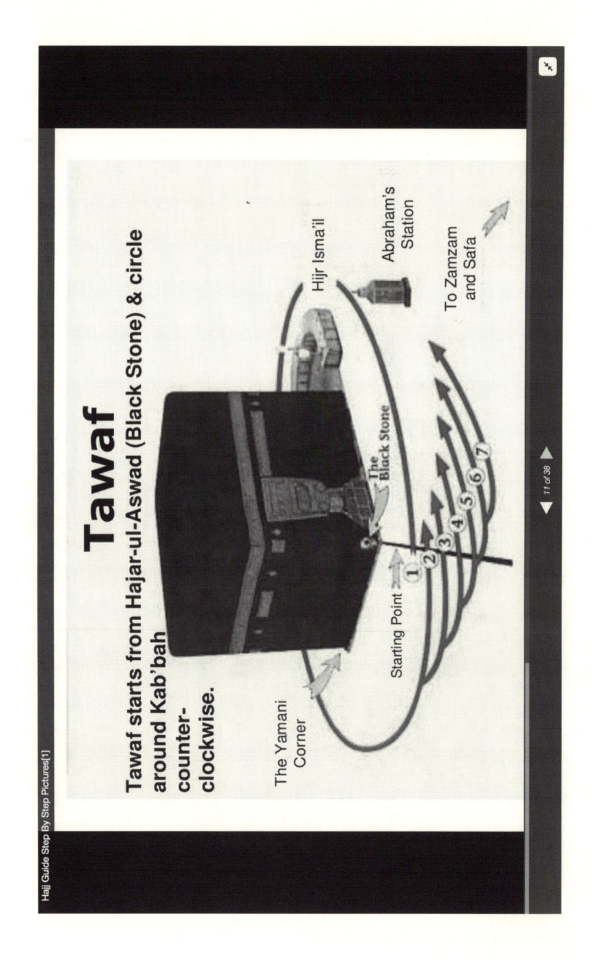

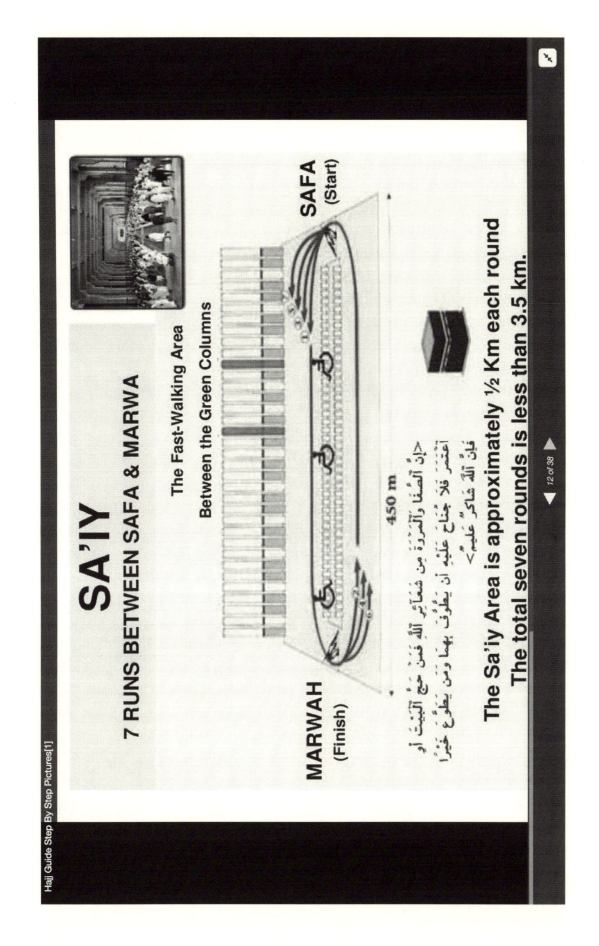

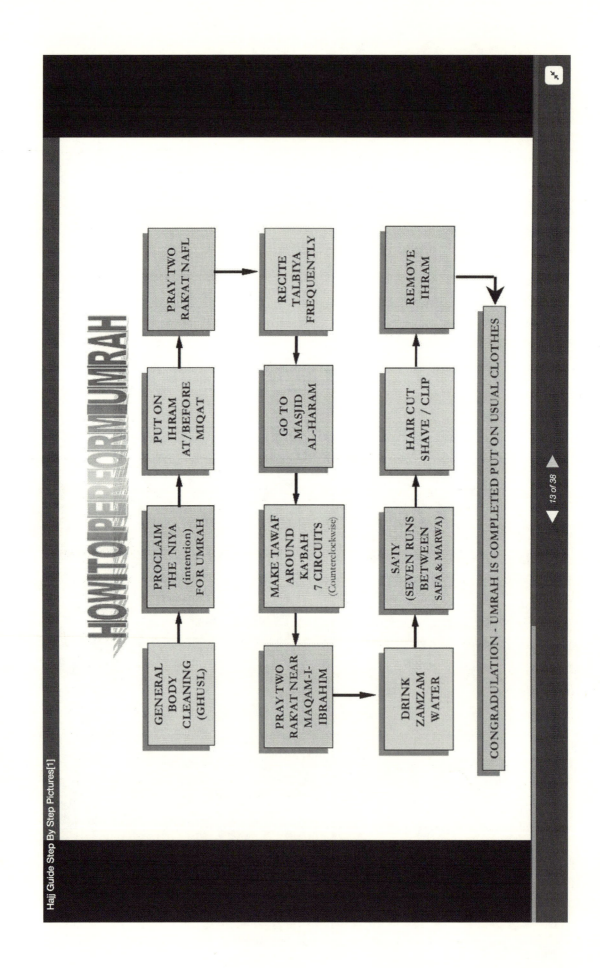

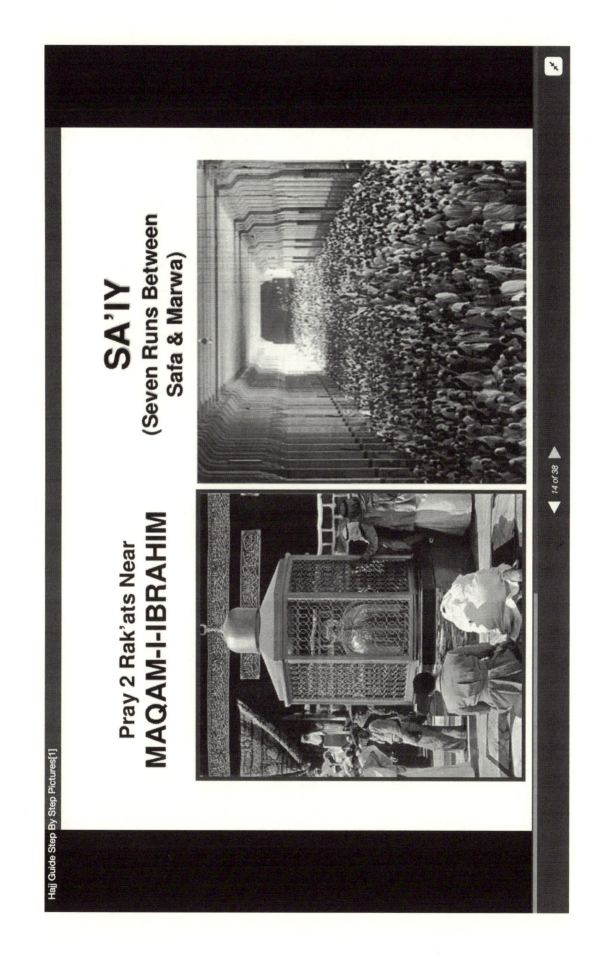

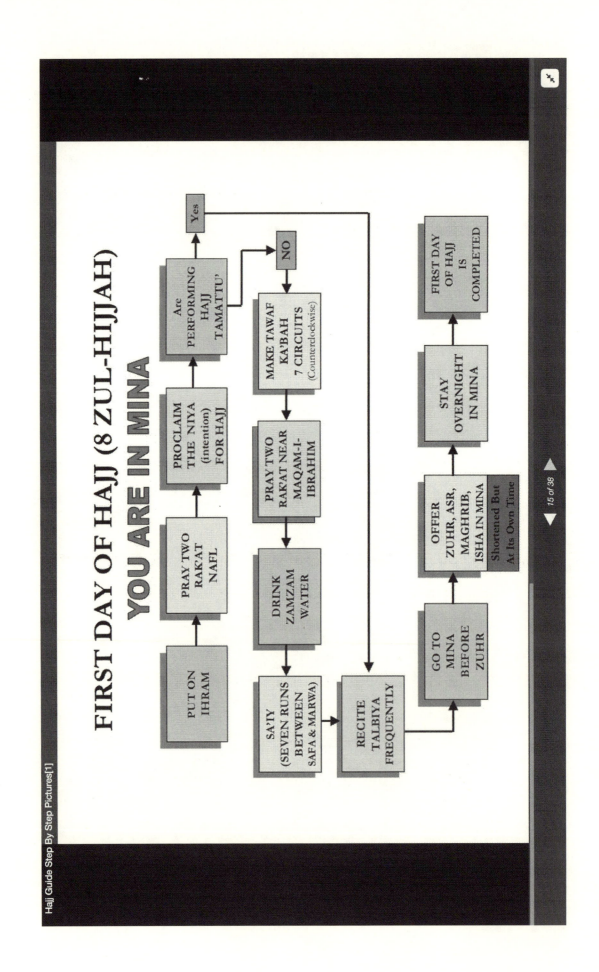

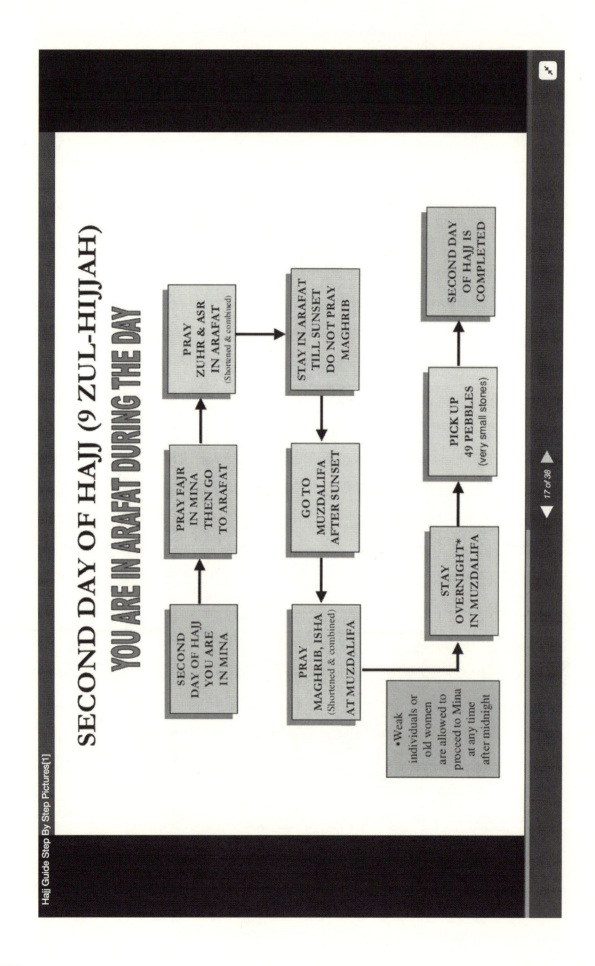

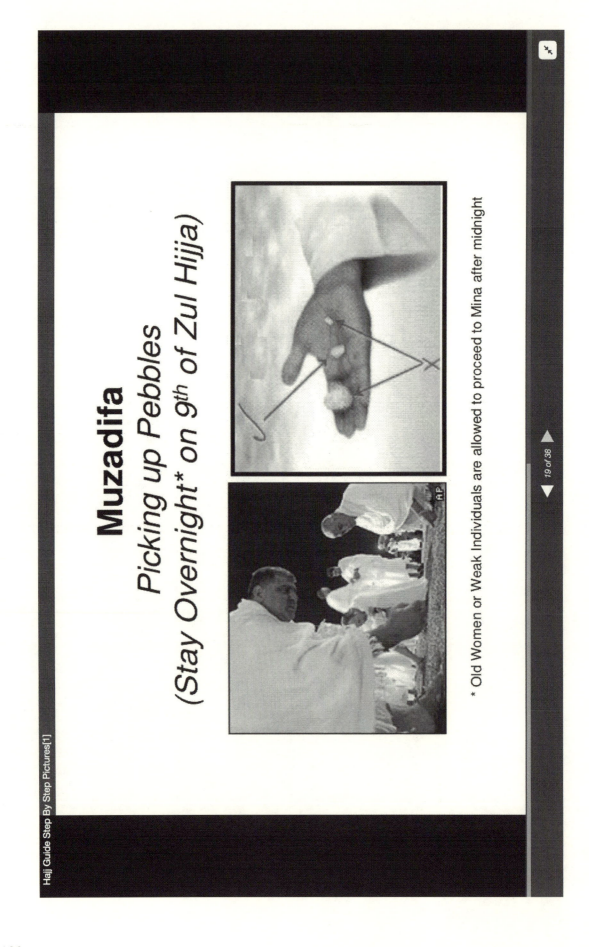

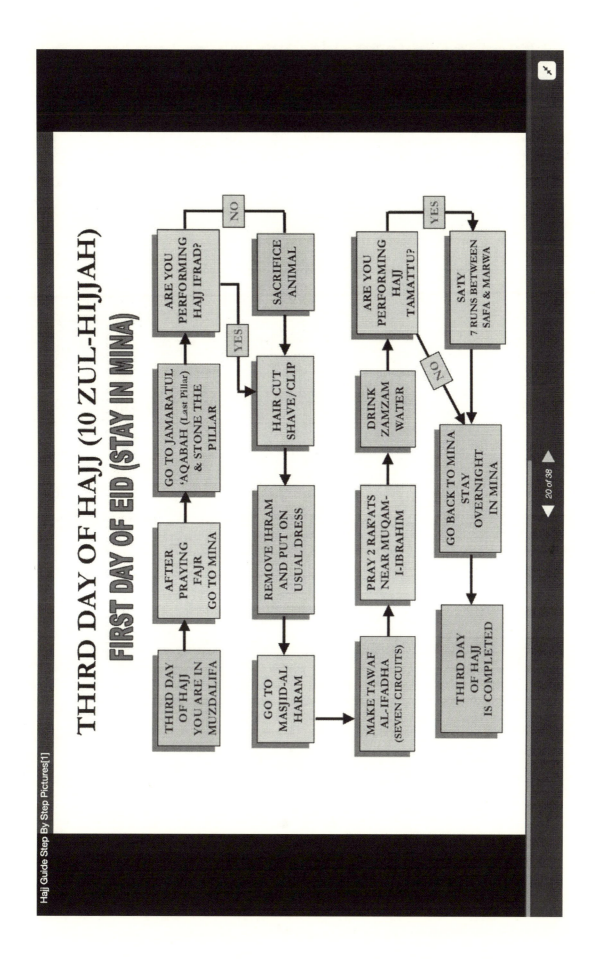

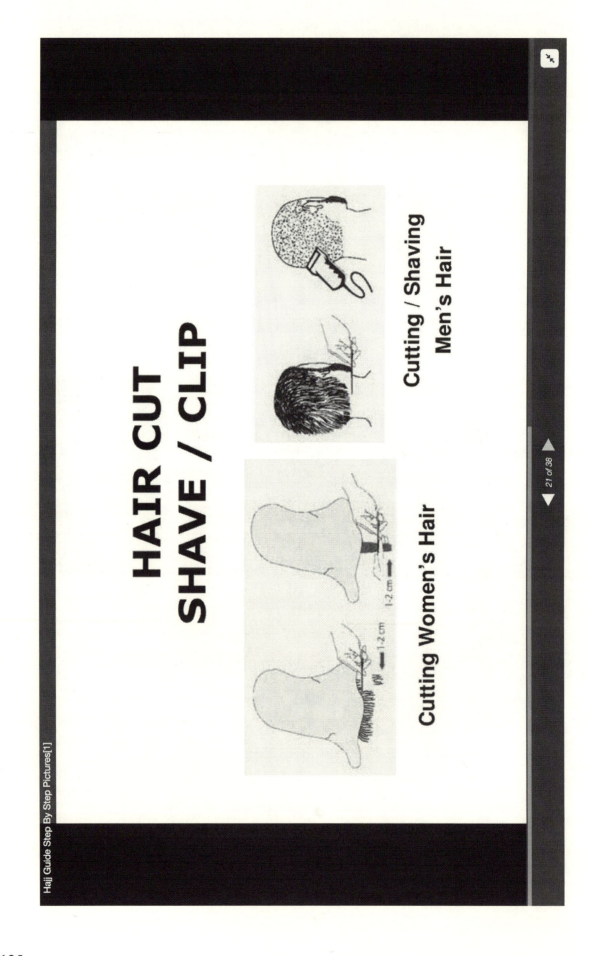

Sacrifice on the Day of Eid

Mina Slaughter House:
Pilgrims can go here to witness their sacrifice

Booths around Makkah and Mina have been set up by the Islamic Development Bank (IDB) to facilitate buying coupons for slaughtering and distributing sacrificial animals.

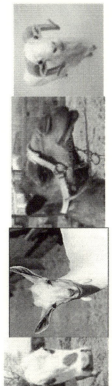

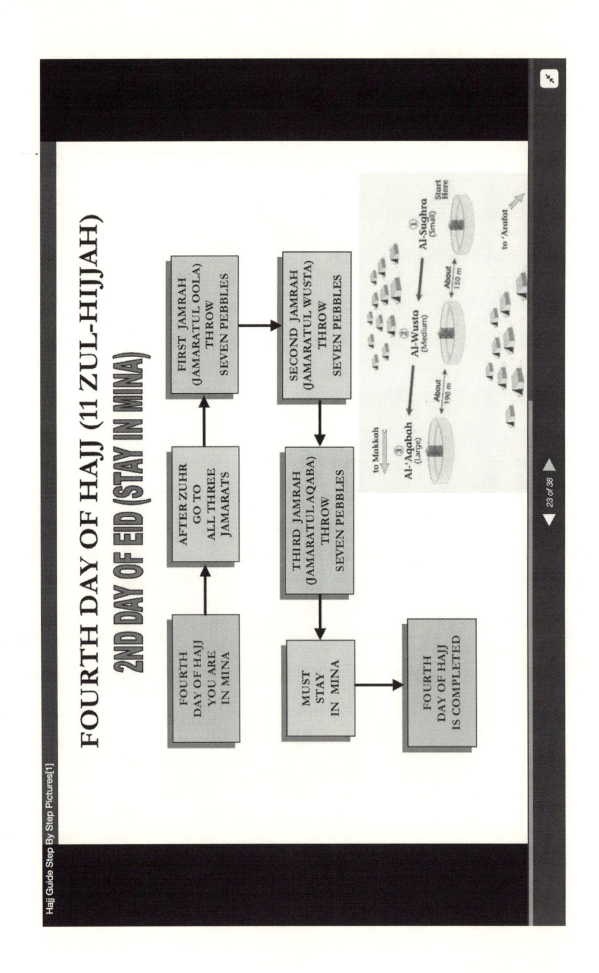

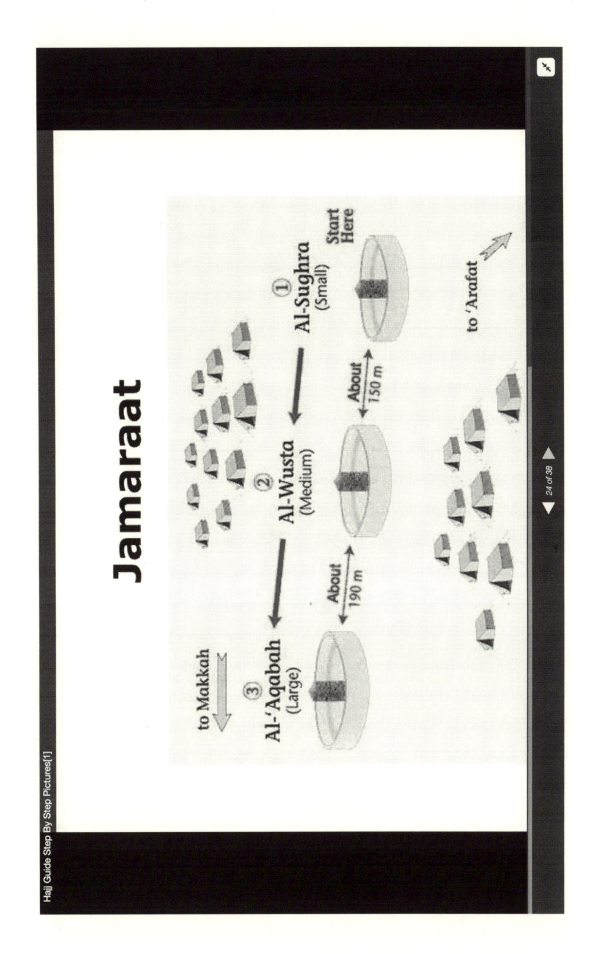

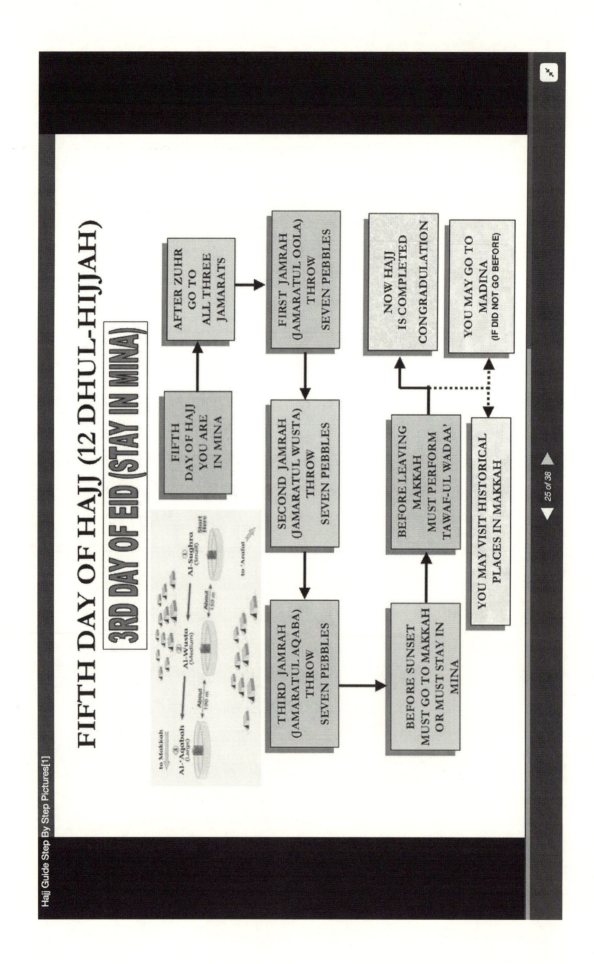

HISTORICAL PLACES OF MAKKAH

Masjid Al-Haram

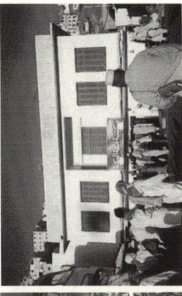

Birth place of Prophet :

The house where the Holy prophet was born is situated in Suq Al-Lail Street. At this place, there exists a library today. If you come out of Haram near Safa hill, this house is about two furlongs away on the right side.

HISTORICAL PLACES OF MAKKAH

The cave of the First Qur'anic Revelation (Cave of Hira) on the Mountain of Light (Jab al Noor)

Cave of Thaur. A cave in the mountain where The Holy Prophet (S.A.W.) and Hadhrat Abu Bakr Siddique(R.A.) took refuge

HISTORICAL PLACES OF MAKKAH

Inside Jannat al-Mualla. Behind the white wall where you see people standing is where the Prophet's [s] family members are buried i.e. Abu Talib [a], Abdul Muttalib [a], Sayyida Khadija [a], etc. Looking through the grilled windows on the wall, one can see a white rectangle on the ground (partially visible in the 2nd pic). This is the grave of Ummul Mu'mineen Sayyida Khadija [a], the wife of the Prophet [s] and mother of Sayyida Fatima az-Zahra [a]

Masjid Shajarah. Not to be confused with the Masjid Shajarah in Madina (Miqat), this is where the Prophet [s] camped when he was stopped by the Meccan leaders from performing Hajj. Thereafter the Treaty of Hudaybiya was signed. This mosque is a little further to the left of Masjid Hudaybiya when coming from Masjid al-Haram

HISTORICAL PLACES OF MAKKAH

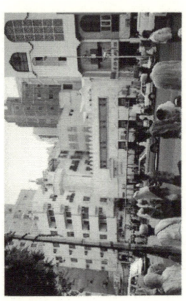

Masjid Hudaybiya. This is where the Treaty of Hudaybiya was signed and where the Meccan leaders asked the words in the treaty "Muhammad Rasulullah" to be replaced with "Muhammad bin Abdullah". This mosque is on the way to Jannat al-Mualla from Masjid al-Haram

Masjid Jinn. The Prophet [s] was reciting the Qur'an here when a group of jinn passing by heard him. They were impressed and converted to Islam. A verse of the Qur'an in Sura Jinn narrates this incident

HISTORICAL PLACES OF MADINA

Masjid - E - Quba

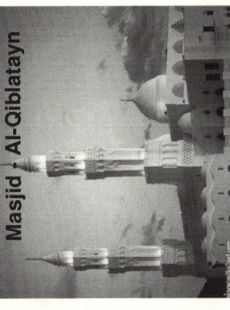

This is the very first mosque of Muslim. The Prophet Muhammad and his companions built it with their own hands. According to authentic Hadith **"To offer 2 Rakaats of Nafl in this Masjid is equal to one Umrah"**

Masjid - Al-Qiblatayn

In this Masjid, Allah (swt) directed Prophet Muhammad (saw) in the middle of a salaat to turn his face from Islam's first Qibla, "Bait-ul-Muqqadis", (Masjid Alaqs in Jerusalem) to "Ka'ba" in "Masjid al-Haram" in Makka. Consequently, this mosque is known as a mosque with two qiblas (Qiblatayn)

HISTORICAL PLACES OF MADINA

Masjid Ghamama

The mosque of clouds derives its name from the occasion when the Prophet prayed for rain and suddenly clouds appeared and rain fell. The mosque is located close to the Masjid al-Nabai (the Prophet's Mosque).

Masjid Juma

It is near Bustan al Jaza in the valley Zanuna to the east on the new road to Quba. The Messenger of Allah prayed the first Friday there.

HISTORICAL PLACES OF MADINA

Janatul Baqi

QABRE-E-HAZRAT IBRAHIM BIN PAYGHMBER MOHAMMAD (P.B.U.H.) (MADINA)

QABRE-E-ABDULLAH BIN JAFER-E-TAYYAR AND AQIL BIN ABU TALIB (MADINA)

HISTORICAL PLACES OF MADINA
Map of Janatul Baqi

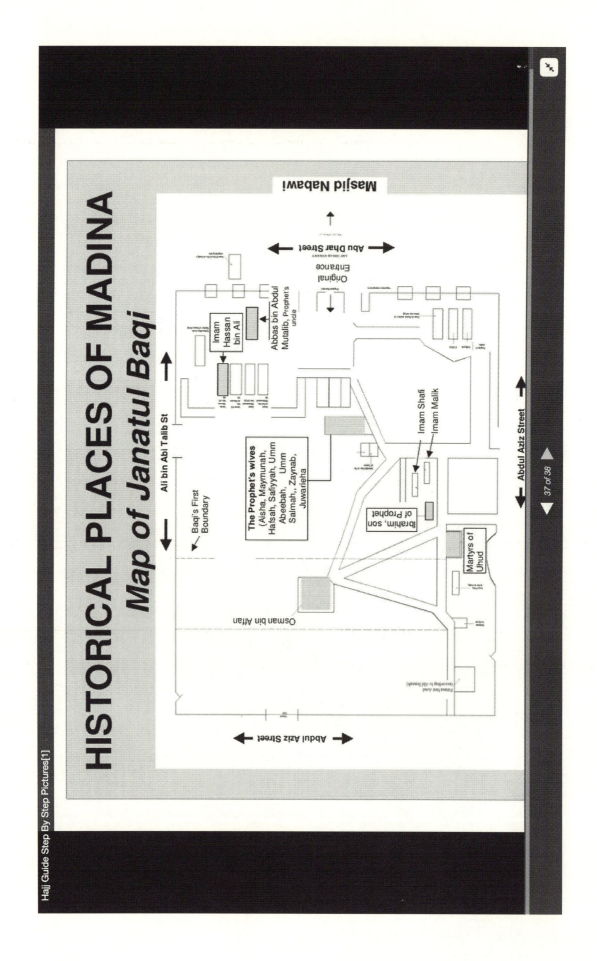

On Establishing Friday Prayers in Prison

QUESTION
Esteemed sir, there is an issue towards which I would like to direct your attention. Is it permissible to pray the Friday prayers in prison? Please provide an answer.

ANSWER
If the government does not forbid it, and has in fact given permission, then you can pray the Friday prayers in prison. Regarding [the issue of] the average citizen being prevented from entering the prison [being a reason for its invalidity], this is an institution restriction [which applies to the entire facility]. It is not there to prevent others from joining the Friday prayer. This is similar to the situation in which Friday prayers are held in forts whose gates have been shut [either] due to fear of the enemy or simply out of habit. It is stated in *Al-Durr al-Mukhtār*,

> [A]nd the seventh [condition for establishing Friday prayer] is open permission…. Closing the door of a fort in fear of an enemy or due to an old habit will not contradict this condition, as an open permission is still in place for its inhabitants. The shutting of the door is simply done to keep out enemies, not with the intent of keeping out worshippers… And it is written in *Al-Shāmiyyah*, "Only [intentionally] preventing worshippers [from attending] will contradict this condition and keeping away enemies will not." [1]

For further information, please see *Fatāwā Maḥmūdiyyah* (Vol. 8, pg 183, Jāmi'ah Farūqiyyah), and *Āḥsan al-Fatāwā* (Vol. 4, pg 112).

And Allah knows best.

- Muftī Raḍā al-Ḥaq and Muftī Muḥammad Ilyās Shaykh.

[Translated from *Fatāwā Darul 'Ulūm Zakariyyā* - Translation checked and approved by Mawlana Abdullah Ayaz Mullanee]

---

[1] *Al- Durr al-Mukhtār* with al-Shāmi (Vol 2, pg 152, Bāb al-Jumu☐ah, Sa'īd Company). This is also mentioned in *Marāqī al-Falāḥ* along with *Ḥāshiyah al- Ṭaḥṭāwī* (pg 510, "Bāb al-Jumu☐ah", Qadīmī)

Information on Tayba Foundation

Tayba's Mission

Our mission is to provide Islamic correspondence courses at the post-secondary level to the incarcerated and formerly incarcerated through our Distance Learning Program. We've seen the transformative value of higher education and are wholeheartedly committed to establishing the processes that enable our students to inherit a contributory role that will facilitate their self-improvement and allow them to reclaim a future, even beyond the walls of the prison.

Tayba's History

The Tayba Foundation was established in 2008 to provide current and formerly incarcerated men and women with quality Islamic education geared towards the refinement of their thinking and behavior, positioning them to transition to society more productively. Although founded in 2008, Tayba's roots began in 2002 when Shaykh Rami Nsour began teaching prisoners via phone, guiding them through classical Islamic texts and answering questions related to their newfound faith. Over the next few years, under the umbrella of the Zaytuna Prison Outreach Program, these students engaged in serious distance learning with Shaykh Rami, learning Theology ('Aqīda), Islamic Jurisprudence (Fiqh), Spirituality (Tazkiya), Character Development (Akhlaq) and other associated disciplines. Those students went through enough learning to be able to teach other inmates.

It was through this effort that both the need for Islamic Education and its positive transformative effect became apparent. Consequently, in 2008, Tayba Foundation was formally established as an independent organization to impart an educational curriculum to inmates, with the underlying goal of spiritual nourishment and character rectification. Tayba Foundation is a registered non-profit 501(c)3 educational and charitable organization located in the San Francisco Bay Area, but serving all states.

Since 2008, Tayba Foundation has:

- Developed an educational curriculum incorporating traditional Islamic knowledge and accounting for special incarcerated Muslim needs, now serving thousands of students.
- We are continually refining our program based on the needs of our students and the feedback we get.
- Developed an administrative infrastructure to assess, enroll, grade and manage student participation.
- Developed processes to comply with rules and requirements of the prison system. We now serve Tayba students in over 250 prisons in over 30 states.
- Facilitated integration into society of released incarcerated Muslim students, through our Re-entry Program.

Other Programs Offered By Tayba

Tayba Foundation believes in human potential. Through thoughtful, well-designed programs, Tayba helps clients acquire the tools needed to unlock human potential and forge a healthy future. The three components of Tayba's program are **Education, Life Skills, and Reentry**.

We are committed to helping those who have been impacted by mass incarceration and we began offering our services with authentic Islamic education to Muslim men and women who are incarcerated. We worked on our curriculum for over a decade to ensure that our students were receiving a quality education despite their circumstances. But, after hearing your stories of pre-incarceration trauma and the difficulties you face upon reentering society, we knew our work wasn't done. So we added to our curriculum a life skills course which is being finalized and will be rolled out this semester. But, we didn't stop there; we also wanted to ensure that once our brothers and sisters re-entered society, they could benefit from our collective knowledge concerning reentry.

Our mission is to keep supporting our students during their incarceration and afterwards. We aim to provide wrap-around reentry services to anyone who comes to us seeking help, including need for: housing, job training and referrals, life skills services, mental health services, legal resources, and substance abuse services.

Education:

Harnessing the power and potential of postsecondary education, Tayba provides clients with postsecondary opportunities in Islamic Education, Higher Education (Degree Programs), and Art Education.

While religious education and other forms of higher education are important and can be factors in rehabilitation and reducing recidivism, there is also a need for practical life skills. Through a series of coaching, peer-mentorship, utilizing existing course programs, and creating courses where needed, Tayba helps develop a track of learning for each individual that suits their reality.

Life Skills:

What are Life Skills all about? They are the abilities we learn to help us approach objectives of everyday life; they are sets of skills which people use to live and to survive. It may sound simple, that they are the things we do to get through life, and some may assume you already know them. But, life skills are something that we must learn in order to progress and grow and it's a lifelong journey.

Tayba recognizes that many clients lack the skills needed to address the ambiguities and difficulties of life. That's why we teach applied life skills needed to navigate the difficulties and complexities of prison and, when released, the free world, by becoming contributing and law abiding citizens.

Finding housing, jobs, and counseling services are a few of the myriad ways we help our students re-integrate into society.

While religious education and other forms of higher education are important and can be factors in rehabilitation and reducing recidivism, there is also a need for practical life skills.

Life skills are attributes, behaviors, plannings, decisions, experience, foresight, education, roadmaps, wellness, social skills, goal setting, character building, critical thinking, financial intelligence, parenting, and more; learning how to overcome substance dependence/addiction, learning how to manage anger, learning how to reform negative thoughts or faulty thinking, learning how to be a friend, learning how to be an employee, learning how to express oneself, learning empathy, and more.

Through a series of coaching, peer-mentorship, utilizing existing course programs, and creating courses where needed, Tayba helps develop a track of learning for each individual that suits their reality.

Our beloved Prophet (pbuh) was the pinnacle of human intelligence with the best of character and the best example of the mastery of life skills; and through learning life skills we will all hopefully become more like him.

If you have any questions about the Life Skills courses, please contact us, especially if you are a group facilitator or mentor, imam/amir, if you lead taleems, etc, as we can help you with additional training to increase your capacity of leading self-help groups. You can reach out to Amir at the Life Skills Department by calling 510-952-9875 or emailing lifeskills@taybafoundation.org. You can also send a letter to:

Tayba Foundation
Attn Life Skills Dept.
P.O. Box 247
Union City, CA 94587

Reentry:

Tayba works with the individual once they are released in a series of coaching and peer-mentoring sessions by checking in with them regularly, offering any tips and advice to increase the success of their reentry, and connecting them with community members who can act as role models.

Our team includes formerly incarcerated individuals who have made a successful reentry into society. Tayba staff gauge successful reentry by the individual not re-offending, getting off parole, having a stable family and job, as well as other factors our team uses to assess each individual case.

We are happy to announce to you that the Tayba Foundation has opened a reentry office in Southern California and has embarked on providing case management and referral services for reentry resources to those impacted by incarceration across the nation.

At this moment, our reentry office work consists of three things: 1) case management and referrals to anyone impacted by incarceration who seeks our help; 2) assisting our students who are close to being released with information on reentry resources in their local areas; 3) also, we are reaching out to Muslim communities nationwide to try to 'plug in' our brothers and sisters to their local support networks and other Islamic resources. Keep us in your prayers and stay tuned for more announcements toward our vision as we continue to work with Allah's help.

If you have been approved for parole within the next 6-12 months, and would like our Reentry coaches to help in your planning or if you are about 3 months from going home, and would like us to assist you with finding resources in your release area, contact us at 510-952-9459 or send us an email at reentry@taybafoundation.org. You can also send a letter to:

Tayba Foundation
Attn Reentry Dept.
P.O. Box 247
Union City, CA 94587

The Tayba Team

Shaykh Rami Nsour, Founding Director & Teacher

Rami Nsour spent a number of years in Mauritania where he studied at some of the foremost Islamic Colleges (*maḥḍaras*). He completed studies in various subjects of Islamic studies and received traditional teaching license (*ijāza*) to transmit what he learned. In addition to his extensive study of Islamic law (*fiqh*), he was afforded an extraordinary 'in-residence' experience to train in answering questions of Islamic faith, law and practice.

Rami has translated traditional Islamic texts, done extensive spiritual counseling and public speaking, and teaches regularly both in-person and online. He co-founded the Tayba Foundation, which is the first organization to offer a distance-learning program in Islamic Education to incarcerated men and women in the United States. He has extensive experience in curriculum development, specifically with character (*akhlāq*). Rami holds a B.A. in Human Development with a focus on Early Childhood and a M.A. in Educational Psychology. Rami resides in the San Francisco Bay Area with his wife and three children.

Nabil Afifi, Fundraising & Development Manager and Co-Founder

Working closely with the Tayba's staff and volunteers, Nabil helps Tayba succeed by implementing and improving existing programs as well as new ones. He also helps develop fundraising activity plans and strategies to increase contributions. Nabil is the Co-Founder of Tayba Foundation and holds a Masters in Public Administration from CSUEB with many years of experience in both business and nonprofit settings. Also, he studied sacred knowledge for 4 years in the seminary of Murabit al Hajj in Mauritania.

About working in Tayba, he enjoys supporting Muslim inmates and their spiritual needs and says, "I pray to Allah ﷻ that He accepts our work…Ameen…At the end, that is all what matters."

Lumumba Shakur, Manager of Academic Affairs

Lumumba Shakur manages Tayba Foundation's academic affairs, including both course and student development. He studied a number of beginning texts in the disciplines of Fiqh, Uṣūl, Ḥadīth, ʿAqīda and logic; all the while supplementing his learning through personal readings, private conversations, and weekend knowledge retreats. He eventually became a volunteer Teaching Assistant at SeekersHub Online, which is how he first met Shaykh Rami Nsour. While serving as a Teaching Assistant for Shaykh Rami, Lumumba helped answer questions posed by his fellow students and assisted Shaykh Rami with the nuts and bolts of the course. This experience naturally morphed into his current role once he was hired with Tayba Foundation.

Lumumba brings that unconventional learning experience to Tayba Foundation. Because of the manner in which he has studied, he understands many of the challenges, frustrations and limitations of distance learning and will, insha Allah, help bring a unique perspective to Tayba Foundation.

About Tayba Foundation and the work they do, he says, "I used to work with youth in residential settings. One of the problems I was routinely faced with were teenage boys who identified as Muslim (many because their fathers converted in prison), but knew almost nothing about the religion. I am humbled, honored and excited at being given the opportunity to work with a population of Muslims who are often forgotten, but who have the potential to become the leaders and pillars of our community. I hope that my past experience has been a training ground that has been preparing me to help Shaykh Rami and the staff at Tayba in their wonderful effort."

Abdul Muhaymin Al-Salim, Instructor

Abdul Muhaymin Al-Salim (Eugene Priester, III) has been a student with the Tayba Foundation since 2013. After converting to Islām in 2004, while serving a dual Federal and State sentence, he sought to have a sound understanding of the Prophetic Model, and after eight years in a Federal Institution without spiritual support for himself and the larger Muslim population, Al-Salim was connected with Shaykh Rami and Tayba Foundation.

Abdul Muhaymin is currently pursuing a Bachelor's degree in Psychology while furthering his studies of the Islamic sciences. Abdul Muhaymin has had the opportunity to study several books in the Tayba curriculum as well as studying other books of 'Aqīda and Ḥadīth and receiving *Ijaza* and is working towards memorizing Sirajus Salik.

He has also started a Consulting and Educational Services company; EP3 & Associates/ Al Qiyaamah, Inc., which focuses on Business, Educational, and Community Development consulting and learning opportunities based on the Islamic model.

About Tayba, he says, "There is no greater feeling than to know that there is a place that provides incarcerated Muslims with a complete package that offers the individual with an outlet to completely transform themselves into outstanding Muslims/Human-Beings. Allah, Subhānahu wa Ta`Ālā, has granted me a tremendous opportunity to gain redemption from my previous path in life by Blessing me with Al-Islām, Al-Ḥamdu-li-Llah. His Tawfīq has manifested by connecting me with Shaykh Rami & the Tayba Foundation, Māshā'Allah, Tabārakallahu `Alaynā fī kulli Khayr.——I am here to serve."

Tabari Abdul-Zahir, Re-entry Manager

Born to Muslim parents in the 1970's, Tabari Abdul-Zahir learned the basics of Islam at a young age. By his late teens, he learned how to read Arabic and was introduced to Islamic law via tertiary fiqh (jurisprudence) texts. It wasn't until his mid twenties that he was able to formally sit with Islamic scholars from West Africa who helped him to learn Aqeedah (Islamic belief system), Fiqh (applied Islamic law), Tazkiyya (spiritual purification) and other Islamic Sciences. Due to a series of bad choices and spiritual heedlessness, Abdul-Zahir found himself in Federal prison for a non-violent drug crime from 2006-2016.

With plenty of time to study and teach, he vigorously delved into the Islamic Sciences with a new sense of purpose and direction. While teaching in prison and trying to develop a consistent method of delivering traditional Islam, Abdul-Zahir heard about the *Tayba Foundation* in 2007 through a family member and was blessed to establish contact with the founders, who sent him the religious texts, while at the same time explaining their traditional method of transmission. Due to having qualified teachers who were on demand, along with their responses to difficult questions and thorny issues, the *Tayba Foundation* was able to facilitate Abdul-Zahir's learning and teaching in an extraordinary fashion. Abdul-Zahir continued to study and teach the *Tayba Foundation* curriculum until released in early 2016.

After release, Abdul-Zahir was able to complete two Associate degrees in the behavioral sciences, a Bachelor's degree in Arabic language, literature and culture and a Master's in Social Work.

The *Tayba Foundation* continued to provide Abdul-Zahir teaching opportunities after his release by encouraging him to use his knowledge of Islam combined with his knowledge of the issues concerning inmates to write a book introducing Islam which would be beneficial to inmates and the larger Muslim community at large. This work was completed at the end of 2017 and is a 240 page work called, 'INTRODUCTION TO ISLAM: With practical examples and advice for Muslims in prison', a.k.a 'Islam 099'.

Due to his Islamic learning via the *Tayba Foundation*, Abdul-Zahir was able to be a teaching resource for various prominent Islamic institutions in Southern California working as a teacher in Arabic, Fiqh, Seerah, and Islamic History. Abdul-Zahir's engagement with these institutions also include lectures and youth counseling.

Currently, Abdul-Zahir is using his Master's of Social Work from California State University, San Bernardino working as a therapist and drug counselor, while directing both the national and local re-entry programs for the *Tayba Foundation* in Southern California. He is also continuing his studies in the Arabic Language at an Islamic seminary outside of Los Angeles.

Fadil Labib, Re-entry Coordinator

Hailing from Chicago, Fadil knows firsthand the struggles our youth and their families face and is determined to make a difference. Fadil Labib has a unique perspective and practical knowledge of the ills of society associated with the realities of life faced by so many that have been affected by and afflicted with the adversities of those worlds. His initial introduction to Tayba was in the Summer of 2014. Today, Fadil serves as Tayba's National Re-entry coordinator and is the first point of contact (and sometimes only) for many men re-entering private life. Fadil is grateful for the many amazing opportunities he has had and loyal friends in his life. In his free time, Fadil enjoys spending time with his family. Fadil continues to study the Legal System and has a passion for cooking. He has his hands in many community-based ventures, yet most dear to his heart is empowering our youth and strengthening families.

Amir Amiri, Life Skills Department Manager

Amir Amiri is a first-generation American-Afghan sociologist who aspires to provide education and educational resources to those who desire. He has been rewarded with a B.A. in Sociology, is a certified WRAP (Wellness Action Recovery Planning) co-facilitator, and more. Amir has been working with Tayba Foundation with incarcerated and formerly incarcerated populations since 2018 and is currently managing the Life Skills Department.

Ustadh Abdul Latif al-Amin, Teacher

Ustadh Abdul Latif al-Amin is a testimony for the passion of seeking knowledge. His story begins between Spokane and Seattle, Washington and the game of basketball. An aspiring young man who just graduated from high school entered North Dakota State University on a basketball scholarship. Majoring in Sports Medicine, it seemed as if his career would fall into place yet he could not ignore a feeling of emptiness inside him. He was introduced to Islam and subsequently converted in September of 1996. "What attracted me to Islam more than anything else was the conduct and the character of the Muslims I met prior to conversion," says Ustadh Abdul Latif as he reflects on his path to Islam.

After spending several years as, what he describes, an "ignorant worshipper," Abdullatif registered for a Deen Intensive program that changed the course of his life. In those blessed days he realized the importance of seeking knowledge in order to personally progress in one's path as a Muslim. Thereafter, he was introduced to SunniPath and enrolled in classes in 2004. As one of the initial students of the new online institution, Abdullatif studied Aqeedah (Belief), Fiqh (Law), Hadith (Prophetic Narrations), Seerah (Biography of the Prophet), and Arabic with Shaykh Faraz Rabbani, Shaykh Omar Qureshi, Shaykh Hamza Karamli, Shaykh Abdul-Kareem Yahya and others. From 2004 to 2009, by Allah's help and divine success, Ustadh Abdullatif was able to complete 45 online courses. He also studied Arabic with local scholars in the Chicago-land area.

Forever a student of knowledge, Ustadh Abdul-Latif is also teaching and assisting with many online classes. He is the Co-Founder of Mercy Islamic Tutoring, an online Islamic Education portal that helps converts and concerned Muslims in general learn the foundational principles of Islam. He is also a researcher for Foundation for Advancement and Development of Education and Learning, where he researches various topics for Islamic Curriculum development. He teaches in his local area in the various Islamic disciplines and gives the Friday sermons. He currently lives in Michigan with his wife and six children. His personal interests include reading about the Prophetic character and stories of the righteous.

Sr. Marianne Hogan (Umm Faisal), Teacher

Marianne Hogan Nsour was born and reared in Mississippi. She participated in the Civil Rights Movement in the 1970's while a college student including the Salad Bowl Boycott in support of the United Farm Workers where she met her late husband, Salameh Abdulhamid Nsour of Salt, Jordan. They lived in Jordan for eleven years and resettled in California in 1991 with their five children. She has worked as an English teacher and real estate agent for many years. Her interests include creative writing and researching the Arabic origins of all languages. She dreams of opening a da'wa center in her hometown of Vicksburg.

Michelle Harmer (Khadija), Program Manager

Michelle's role as Program Manager involves overseeing the development of the unique Islamic studies curriculum that Tayba offers to incarcerated men and women. As a part of helping students attain success with Tayba, Michelle is working on developing student tracking, and implementing best practice in all aspects of Tayba's courses. Michelle also lends a hand in other Tayba projects including development and outreach.

Michelle holds a BA (Hons) in Retail Marketing and a Professional Diploma in Marketing from the Chartered Institute of Marketing (UK). Originally from Britain, Michelle embraced Islām in 2004. She is married and currently lives in Toronto, Canada.

Kelly Légère-Gallant, Program Coordinator

Kelly works as our Program Coordinator, offering administrative support to the Academy team members and to other Tayba projects when needed. Kelly is a certified, bilingual (EN/FR) Educational Assistant and she has specialized training to help students with different types of learning difficulties. As an EA, she helps students understand course materials as well as assisting students in managing their learning challenges through direct or indirect guidance.

Kelly acquired her *fard 'ayn* knowledge in Mālikī Fiqh and hopes to further advance in her Islamic studies; especially in the Arabic language.

About working with Tayba, she says, "It is truly a blessing to be part of the Tayba team and I am very happy to be of service to the Ummah, especially to be helping the Students of Tayba Foundation. I see it as my duty to put my natural talents and skills to use for an excellent cause. May Allah accept these works from us all and forgive our shortcomings. May we all benefit from it. May Allah ﷻ bless our teachers and those seeking knowledge. Amīn."

Tayba's Educational Program

We offer two Study Terms per year. Our **Spring Term** runs from March 1 to June 30 and our **Fall Term** runs from September 1 to December 31, offering students the chance to study year-round.

Our curriculum is designed to ensure that all the course work fits into a specific theme of character reformation. We believe that character reformation is the key to not only working with current or formerly incarcerated men and women, but also to their eventual release and reintegration into the greater society.

Our curriculum incorporates a significant amount of spiritual and behavioral modification geared towards developing qualities which increase accountability for actions. These components of our curriculum are thoroughly reinforced throughout all the courses.

The three core components of the program are:

1) Sound Islamic knowledge
2) Realization of the prisoner's experience
3) Recognition of prison guidelines

Key Highlights of the Curriculum:
• Emphasis on character development influences our choice of texts
• Students learn the essentials of their faith (farḍ ʿayn)
• An opportunity to learn the Arabic Language
• Emphasis on recognizing and respecting differences of opinion
• Students are required to write an essay that speaks about how the course affected them at the personal, familial and communal level
• Students have a base for meaningful reflection and spiritual development
• Draws upon methodology and texts used in many Islamic centers of higher learning.

Current courses offered and their prerequisites

Below is a list of the courses we currently offer. Please note that the courses are designed to be taken in a particular order, which means you must pass certain courses before you can take others. This is to help you along a path of learning which will give you the best chance of success.

Your Journey
Through Tayba's Curriculum

INTRO LEVEL

 **ISLAM99** — Introduction to Islam → **IMAN100** — Beliefs of a Muslim → **FIQH100** — How to Approach Studying Fiqh

100 LEVEL STAGE 1

 FIQH101/111/121* — Prayer & Purification →  **ADAB101** — Rights of Parents →  **FIQH102/112/122*** — Five Pillars

 ADAB102 — Prohibitions of the Tongue → **IHSN101** — Introduction to Purification of the Heart

*FIQH classes are offered in the Maliki, Hanafi & Shafii schools of Islamic Law.

 QRAN101 — Introduction to Quran → **HDTH101** — Introduction to Hadith → **USUL101** — Introduction to Usul → **SIRA101** — Prophetic Biography

100 LEVEL STAGE 2

 IMAN101 — Introduction to Islamic Theology → Final Assignment & Completion of 100-Level

Course assignments

All assignments are "open book" and so you may use your book and notes. Before starting an exam, you should study the material as thoroughly as you would for a closed-book exam in a classroom. There is no time limit for the exam.

We request that you write all assignments in print, and do not use cursive handwriting. **USE BLUE OR BLACK INK ONLY.** While we encourage those of you who can write in cursive to keep up this skill, it is much easier to grade your assignments if you write only in legible print.

Your grade will be based on the number of points you earn on the assignments. Submit everything together.

INCLUDE YOUR NAME AND ID NUMBER ON ALL ASSIGNMENTS.

DO NOT SUBMIT ASSIGNMENTS SEPARATELY.

DO NOT SUBMIT INCOMPLETE WORK. THIS TAKES A LOT OF OUR OFFICE TIME TO NOTIFY YOU OF WHAT IS MISSING. PLEASE SUBMIT A COMPLETE PACKET AND IF YOU CANNOT, THEN WAIT UNTIL YOU CAN.

The final deadline to submit both exams and all assignments is **June 30** for the Spring Term and **December 31** for the Fall Term.

Please note that any assignment received AFTER the due date will NOT be read. It will be refused and will only be graded the next semester. This is to assist our graders in grading assignments in a timely fashion, as a better service to our students. We ask that you please respect the deadlines.

If, for any reason, you are unable to submit the coursework on time, please provide a brief note *with as much notice as possible* (before the deadline) explaining the reason for late submission and we will evaluate the eligibility of a late submission at that time.

Course Assignments Checklist:

❏ I read/studied the coursebook before submitting my assignments.
❏ I have asked any questions I have about the course material before submitting my assignments OR the questions I have about the course material are being submitted on a seperate piece of paper, seperate from my written assignments (if applicable).
❏ I have read all of the assignments and understand what I need to do.
❏ I contacted Tayba to clarify any questions I might have about the assignments (if applicable).
❏ I completed all assignments using blue or black ink only.
❏ I completed the written assignments by printing clearly and legibly.
❏ I checked my work for spelling, grammar, punctuation and accuracy before submitting it to Tayba.
❏ I made a copy of my written assignments for my records (recommended, but not necessary).
❏ I included my name and ID number on all of my assignments.
❏ I am submitting all of my assignments together in one packet.
❏ I am submitting my assignments before the deadline (June 30 for Spring/December 31 for Fall).

Assignment #1: Essay

We learned in Akhdari that it is obligatory to learn the ruling of something before trying to implement it. **Reflect back on your own personal learning path and that of your community and speak about instances where not knowing the proper ruling has caused a problem(s). Also give examples of instances where the community not knowing the comprehensive ruling of something resulted in unnecessary fitna and how what you have learned since finishing FIQH 102 could have helped resolve the situation.**

The paper can be anywhere from 5-10 pages typed or handwritten. Make sure to double space between lines. If you will be writing the paper by hand, you should make sure to write as clearly as you can. Please write in print for handwritten papers. Make sure to write in pen, not pencil, unless you do not have access to a pen. If your handwriting is small, please write a little larger for this paper.

Do not be intimidated by this paper. We are not trying to assess your essay skills, grammar, punctuation, spelling, etc. Those are important and you should work on them, but you will be graded only on content. To help you understand what we are looking for in your essay, the table below shows how your essay will be graded:

Area to be graded	Completed	Points available	Total points
Paper is 5-10 pages	Yes [ ] No [ ]	4	
Clear handwriting	Yes [ ] No [ ]	3	
Paper is written in pen or typed	Yes [ ] No [ ]	2	
Demonstrates understanding of the text and how to apply it	Yes [X] No [ ]	16	
Total points		25	

Assignment #2: Compare & Contrast

Part of the reason for the assignments to give you is to help make sure you sufficiently study the text and are able to understand and explain it to others. *Tuhfat al-Mubtadi* was written for beginners and keeps the subjects limited to the essentials. **Now that you have studied *Maraqi al-Sada`at* that is a little more detailed, mention the things you learned in each section from *Maraqi al-Sada`at* that you would add to your explanation of *Tuhfat al-Mubtadi* if you were teaching to a beginner's fiqh class. Please identify the sections from *Tuhfat al-Mubtadi* only and limit yourself to only mentioning those things that you think are important for them to know from *Maraqi al-Sada`at*. But please justify the reason why you have included them.** NOTE: There is no need for you to give a detailed commentary on the actual masa'il (legal issues) that you have identified.

Assignment #3: Fasting Pamphlet

For this project, you will demonstrate your **knowledge on fasting from this course**. You can do this in a number of ways and here are some suggestions:

- You are going to introduce a new Muslim to the rules of fasting and zakat. You write him a lengthy letter detailing the main points that he or she should be aware of.
- You create a pamphlet about the main points for a new Muslim or a newly practicing Muslim should know.
- Any other method that you feel will show us that you have a solid understanding of fasting and zakat.

NOTE: Do not simply copy out the points from the course. The point of this project is for you to present the material from the course in a NEW manner. You are not changing the material, but you are changing the method in which the transmission is occurring. Also note that points will be taken off for rulings mentioned that either reflect a different scholarly opinion than what was mentioned in or fail to include important rulings from the course book.

Assignment #4: Zakat Pamphlet

For this project, you will demonstrate your **knowledge on zakat from this course**. You can do this in a number of ways, again here are some suggestions:

- You are going to introduce a new Muslim to the rules of fasting and zakat. You write him a lengthy letter detailing the main points that he or she should be aware of.
- You create a pamphlet about the main points for a new Muslim or a newly practicing Muslim should know.
- Any other method that you feel will show us that you have a solid understanding of fasting and zakat.

NOTE: Do not simply copy out the points from the course. The point of this project is for you to present the material from the course in a NEW manner. You are not changing the material, but you are changing the method in which the transmission is occurring. Also note that points will be taken off for rulings mentioned that either reflect a different scholarly opinion than what was mentioned in or fail to include important rulings from the course book.

Assignment #5: Hajj Diary

For this project, you will demonstrate your knowledge on hajj. You can do this in a number of ways and here are some suggestions:

- You have made it to hajj (keep your hopes alive, anything can happen, even if you have life without parole-Allah is able to change things). You are keeping a diary of your whole experience. You keep a day by day account on what you are doing throughout the hajj mentioning all the main points of what you will be doing.
- You could choose to "write a letter home" from your hajj about what you did. Think about the letter El Hajj Malik El Shabazz wrote. This would be like it, only with more fiqh details on the day to day of what you did.
- A chart or graph that you will give to someone going on Hajj. If you choose this project, do not copy what was done in the slides that I have included in this packet.

*** EXTRA CREDIT *** Assignment #6: Scenario Questions *** EXTRA CREDIT ***

Instructions: Read the scenario carefully and write out your answer on a separate piece of paper. You do not have to rewrite the questions. Please just write "Scenario Questions v.3" at the top of your paper. **Make sure to include all of the information needed to fully answer the question.** This assignment has been changed to an optional extra credit assignment. Every question is worth a potential point towards your final grade. **Each question has two parts: (A) your answer and (B) your justification each worth half a point. Your justification should *include* a specific reference to the relevant line or commentary in the coursebook *as well as* an explanation of the legal principle(s)/reasoning underlying your answer.** The citation and explanation are each worth half a point. **There is also only one solution to each of these questions.** If you give more than one solution the entire question would be marked as incorrect.

1)   Anthony wakes up in the morning from a wet dream and notices a dry white substance in his underwear. The showers do not open up until 6 am. He has a sink in his cell, but he also has a roommate. He got permission to keep a small smooth stone for tayammum from the chaplain. He cannot wait until hygiene time to make ghusl in the showers without missing the prayer. **(A) How should he perform tahara to catch Fajr? (B) Justify your answer.**

2)   Jose's family sent him a pair of waterproof hiking socks in the mail. Jose took a shower in the morning, made his wudu, and then got dressed wearing his new socks. A few hours later he had the urge to relieve himself, so he used the bathroom and renewed his wudu while wiping over his socks. As Jose left his cellblock, one of the COs told Jose that another prisoner claimed Jose had threatened him with a homemade knife and he therefore needed to comply with a strip search. Jose complied, removed all of his clothing (socks included), was searched, cleared, and allowed to proceed with what he was doing. Once he got to the chapel, he entered the bathroom and washed only his feet. He then entered the designated musalla and joined the congregational prayer. **(A) Was Jose's prayer valid? (B) Justify your answer.**

3)   Joshua was studying fiqh and came to the passage that explained that "freedom" was one of the conditions of Jumu`a. He reasoned that since he was a prisoner, he did not meet the condition of freedom. He still attended Jumu`a with everyone else, but prayed Dhuhr on his own afterwards. There are 50 Muslims in his compound, but no more than 20 inmates are allowed to participate in religious services at

any given time. **(A) Was Joshua correct in his analysis? [½ point] Are there any other conditions that he did not consider that are relevant to his situation? [½ point]? (B) Justify your answer.**

4) Sumayyah's menstruation cycle normally lasts 7 days. However, she took some medication which has affected her menstruation cycle. She bled for 4 days this time and then bleeding stopped completely. It unexpectedly returned 11 days later and she bled for 5 more days. During the second incident of bleeding, she participated in a tajwid class with Auntie Fatima from the local Masjid. Fatima studied fiqh at Al-Azhar in Egypt. Sumayyah was unclear about what to do and so she asked Auntie Fatima after class. **(A) What did Auntie Fatima tell her about her irregular bleeding? (B) Justify your answer.**

5) It is Ramadan. Abdullah, Zayd, and Matthew all have a court appearance scheduled at 10 am. Fajr enters at 5 am and sunrise is at 7 am. The courthouse is two hours away and the transport bus leaves at 6 am. Since they are travelling later, Zayd decides before Fajr that he is not going to fast and ate lunch later at the courthouse. Abdullah and Matthew kept their fasts. Once they all were on the bus and crossed the city line, Abdullah broke his fast and ate the breakfast that the COs were holding for him. Matthew tells both of them that they should not have broken their fast and kept fasting even though several people told him the night before that it was sunna to break the fast while travelling. **(A) Who was correct? (B) Justify your answer. NOTE: The explanation portion of this answer must include an analysis of the position of each individual in the question in order to receive full credit. You will receive ½ a point if your defense of the correct party is sound and ½ a point if your explanation of the other two individual's errors is correct. Your explanations must still include a citation.**

6) Noora is working in the kitchen during lunch and she is in charge of cooking the main course: beef stew. The beef in the stew is neither certified halal nor certified kosher. After Noora finishes preparing the stew, she brings the first batch to the line and informs her co-workers that she is going to take a short break and pray in the back for 5 minutes. Noor prays Dhuhr and as she is reciting her post-prayer dhikr, notices that she had spilled some beef stew on her pants about the size of her fist. She was in such a hurry to get back to work that she did not notice the stain when she was removing the apron to pray and assumed the wetness was from the water she splashed on herself when she was washing the pots in the back. **(A) Is Noora's prayer valid? (B) Justify your answer.**

7) It is near the end of Ramadan and Muhammad's community is in a bit of a crisis about whether or not tomorrow is Eid. Saudi Arabia declared the end of Ramadan to be tomorrow (Friday) and so when

Friday came one group of brothers broke their fast and prayed Eid among themselves. This decision was a bit controversial since some countries claimed Saudi had broken their fast early. The ISNA calendar that had been donated by the local Masjid had determined that Friday was still Ramadan so group of brothers continued fasting, as did the brothers who relied only on physical sighting since the moon had not yet been seen. That Friday evening, the sky was cloudy all over North America and so the moon was not sighted. However, the calendar declared Eid to be Saturday and so when Saturday came the brothers who relied on calculations broke their fast. This decision was also controversial to some. And finally that Saturday night the moon was sighted and so the third set of brothers broke their fast and prayed Eid among themselves on Sunday. The Eid banquet was scheduled for Monday and so even though the community prayed on three different days, everyone celebrated Eid together at the communal banquet. **(A) Muhammad has been studying FIQH 112 with one of the group of brothers, so did he pray Eid on Friday, Saturday, or Sunday? (B) Justify your answer.**

8) Michelle is a new convert and this is her first Ramadan. She started the month fasting, but for the last 4 days she has been on her hayd. Thursday morning before Fajr she checks for purity and does not see its signs. She reads from her Qur'an translation and does a dhikr she was encouraged to do on her hayd in place of prayer. She had gotten used to fasting, so she was not hungry and decided to skip breakfast. A little later in the morning when she is answering the call of nature, she notices that her bleeding seems to have stopped. So she checks for her usual sign of purity, and sees a white discharge so goes to the showers to make ghusl. When her roommate Tiffany notices her appearance, she informs her that since it is Ramadan and she did not yet eat, she is obliged to start fasting. Iman overhears Tiffany, interjects and tells Michelle that fasting is not valid in her situation. However, she still cannot eat since it is Ramadan and has to perform something called "imsak." A little later on, Michelle runs into Shanice who offers her some cookies. Michelle declines and tells Shanice what she was told by the other two ladies. Shanice tells Michelle that both ladies were incorrect and she should go ahead and eat the cookies. **(A) Which of the women was correct? (B) Justify your answer.**

9) It is Ramadan and Abd al-Latif is fasting. He is doing his morning routine and forgot to brush his teeth after suhur. So he grabs his toothbrush, squeezes on a drop of toothpaste, and begins to lift it to his mouth. His roommate Henry sees him, yells "Stop!" and tells Abd al-Latif that he read that he should not brush his teeth with toothpaste during the day of Ramadan. Abd al-Latif tells Henry that he will be careful not to swallow and proceeds to brush his teeth against his roommate's advice. Sure enough, just as Henry feared, Abd al-Latif accidentally swallows some of the toothpaste. Since he broke his fast by

accident, Abd al-Latif reasoned that it is okay for him to go ahead and eat, so goes to breakfast. When he returns to his cell, Henry is waiting on Abd al-Latif with a copy of *Ascent to Felicity* with his finger on a particular line and explains to him how it applies to Abd al-Latif's situation. **(A) What line did Henry show to Abd al-Latif? [½ point] How does it apply to Henry's situation? [½ point] (B) What, if anything, is Abd al-Latif required to do to amend for his mistake?**

10) Jennifer is in prison for armed robbery and vehicular theft. One night she went on a small crime spree, robbed a few small businesses, went home with $5,000 dollars and a car worth $8,000 from a gas station attendant at gunpoint. She did not harm anyone. Jennifer was eventually caught, the car was returned, but only $2,000 of the cash was recovered. Jennifer laundered the rest of the money by depositing it into an account in her mother's name. Shortly after the crime, Jennifer's mother passed away and Jennifer inherited $7,000 of her mother's savings, the remaining $3,000 of stolen cash, a small house worth $90,000, and a brand new car worth $25,000. Before she was incarcerated, she made her sister Nina her power of attorney so that Nina could guard her property and money while she was away. Nina moved into the house and used the money in Jennifer's account to pay the property taxes with Jennifer's permission. Jennifer was introduced to Islam for the first time in prison and took her Shahadah in the 3rd year of her 7 year prison sentence. A little later in the year, the chaplain held a class on zakat and explained to Jennifer how it is supposed to be calculated. That particular year the silver nisba was $300 and the gold nisab was $4,500. Nina also had spent $2,700 from Jennifer's account on taxes. That evening after the ta'leem, Jennifer called Nina and told her to withdraw a certain amount of money. **(A) How much does Jennifer tell Nina to withdraw? [½ point] Who did she tell Nina to give it to? [½ point] (B) Justify your answer.**

P.O. Box 247 Union City, CA 94587

info@taybafoundation.org

www.taybafoundation.org

(510) 952-9683

Student Question Form

Use this form to submit any questions you have about the course material to the Tayba instructors throughout the semester. Please print legibly, print in pen (blue or black only). If you need more space, staple only 8.5x11 size sheets to this form or make copies of this form. **In order to ensure your questions are answered in a timely manner, please return this form to us as soon as you finish reading the coursebook and do not wait until you finish your other assignments so we are not overwhelmed with questions at the end of the semester.** <u>This form is not for submitting your course assignments, it is for submitting your questions to us.</u>

Date: _____

Student name:	ID #:
Name of Institution:	Address:

Course number:	Book title:	Instructor/Commentator:

Question (s):

| Student name: | Course number: |

Question (s):

Question Form for Distance Learning Course

Please write legibly, print in pen (blue or black only). If you need more space staple only 8.5x11 size sheets to this form or make copies of this form. In order to ensure your questions are answered in a timely manner, please return this form to us as soon as you finish reading the coursebook and do not wait until you finish your other assignments so we are not overwhelmed with questions at the end of the semester.

Date: _____

Student name:	ID #:
Name of Institution:	Address:

Course number:	Book title:	Instructor/Commentator:

Question (s):

| Student name: | Course number: |

Question (s):

Question Form for Distance Learning Course

Please write legibly, print in pen (blue or black only). If you need more space staple only 8.5x11 size sheets to this form or make copies of this form. In order to ensure your questions are answered in a timely manner, please return this form to us as soon as you finish reading the coursebook and do not wait until you finish your other assignments so we are not overwhelmed with questions at the end of the semester.

Date: _____

Student name:	ID #:
Name of Institution:	Address:

Course number:	Book title:	Instructor/Commentator:

Question (s):

Student name:	Course number:

Question (s):

Made in United States
Orlando, FL
30 March 2025

59987144R00102